MEANING AND SOURCES OF HUMAN RIGHTS

MEANING AND SOURCES OF HUMAN RIGHTS

GOPAL BHARGAVA

Publications

KALPAZ PUBLICATIONS

DELHI–110052

MEANING AND SOURCES OF HUMAN RIGHTS
(Human Rights)

Rs. 720

ISBN: 9788178352145

Published in 2003 in India by
Kalpaz Publications
C-30, Satyawati Nagar
Delhi-110052
E-mail: kalpaz@hotmail.com

Laser Typesetting at: Varsha Graphics, Delhi
Printed at: Mehra Offset Press, Delhi

Contents

Preface

All human beings are born free and equal in dignity and rights. They are endowed with reason and conscience and should act towards one another in a spirit of brotherhood. The concepts embodied in current human rights documents come from many different traditions, countries and cultures. Religious systems as well as recent movements such as feminism, socialism and environmentalism have also influenced rights and conventions. Many of these influences have conflicting values and there is no agreed way to resolve these so as to identify a "human right" other than the process of negotiation which exists between countries in the development of conventions, declarations and treaties.

While the meaning of human rights is the subject of some debate, the sources of current human rights law is generally accepted. The original source document for current human rights is the *United Nations Declaration of Human Rights*, adopted in 1948 by the majority of the international community in response to the abuses of human rights perpetrated before and during the Second World War. It expresses basic human rights in general terms as a common standard of achievement for all peoples and all nations. These rights include the prevention of slavery and torture, the right to be treated equally regardless of race or gender, the right to own property and the right to privacy.

The covenant which has proved most influential in the development of human rights law has been the *International Covenant on Civil and Political Rights* (the ICCPR). *International Covenant on Economic, Social and Cultural Rights (ICESCR)*, also adopted in 1966. The *ICESCR* provides for the right to be free from hunger, the right to education, the right to social security, the right to physical and mental health and the right of groups to enjoy their own culture and participate in cultural life.

Apart from the *United Nations Declaration on Human Rights* and the *ICCPR*, some of the conventions which have had an influence on the development of Human rights are: The Convention on the Rights of the Child; The International Convention on the Elimination of Racial Discrimination; The Convention on the Elimination of all forms of Discrimination Against Women; The Convention Relating to the Status of Refugees; and United Nations Draft Declaration on the rights of Indigenous Peoples.

This book examines the meaning and sources of "human rights", including the relevant international covenants. This will be a valuable reference tool for all who concerned with human rights issues.

Editor

1

Introduction

The concept of human rights has cultural, moral, religious and social dimensions and a theoretical background that goes back at least as far as the writings of political philosophers such as John Locke in the 17 th century. Human rights are those rights that are universal across all nations. They are based upon the belief that each individual should be treated with the dignity and respect to which, as a human being, they are entitled. One way to define "human rights" then, is that they are part of what each person needs to be human. Human rights, defined in conventions and legislation, are an attempt to express how people's humanity should be respected by those with power over them, particularly governments.

The World War II saw atrocities against populations on an unprecedented scale. One of the most significant responses to the abuses which occurred during was the agreement among nations which came to be known as the Universal Declaration of Human Rights. Since the Declaration was made in 1948 there have been many new international covenants and treaties and the development of a body of international and domestic human rights law. The *United Nations Declaration on Human Rights* encapsulates this in its first two articles:

> All human beings are born free and equal in dignity and rights. They are endowed with reason and conscience and should act towards one another in a spirit of brotherhood. Everyone is entitled to all the rights and freedoms set forth in this Declaration, without distinction of any kind, such as race, colour, sex, language, religion, political or other opinion, national or social origin, property, birth or other status. These rights are given expression in different forms in the various humans rights declarations, treaties and covenants. Thus there are

— 'civil and political rights' — such as rights to life, liberty, free speech, movement, political thought and religious practice, a fair trial, privacy, to found a family and to vote;

— 'economic, social and cultural rights' — such as rights to adequate food and water, health care, education, a clean environment, to respect for cultural practices, and to welfare assistance;

— humanitarian rights — that is the rights of those who are involved in, or affected by, armed conflict, such as the treatment of prisoners of war, of the wounded or sick or shipwrecked, of civilians, and of women and children in particular;

— various categories of rights as defined by the nature of the holders — such as the rights of workers, women, children, minority groups, refugees, indigenous peoples, and people with a disability.

Typically, "First Generation" rights are expressed as individual civil and political rights, and are those most familiar to Western democracies. "Second Generation rights" are economic, social and cultural rights, as exemplified by the International Covenant of Economic Social and Cultural Rights (ICESCR). The rights are primarily concerned with matters such as housing, clothing, food, education and social security, which the individual or group requires to enjoy these rights fully. "Third Generation rights" in contrast derived from developing countries and those with Socialist governments, who saw the rights of "groups" as being overlooked by the traditional focus on individual liberties.

Human Rights, despite being universal, have limits. Rights such as the right to be free from torture or slavery, are generally considered to be absolute, but most other rights have been subject to qualification or limitation in some way. The most important limits on human rights are:

— The generality with which rights are expressed in conventions

— Limitation clauses within individual rights; and

— Limits caused by competing rights

The generality of the expression of rights is a product of how they have developed and how they are agreed upon. The so-called "first generation" human rights were heavily influenced by liberal political philosophy with its emphasis on the individual and their rights against the state. The formulation of the rights owed much to both the Common Law in English-speaking countries and the Civil Law system applying in European countries.

However human rights have come to encompass other influences, particularly with the so-called second and third generation rights.

The concepts embodied in current human rights documents come from many different traditions, countries and cultures. Religious systems such as Christianity, Judaism and Islam have also influenced the concepts behind human rights, while more recent movements such as feminism, socialism and environmentalism have also influenced rights and conventions. Many of these influences have conflicting values and there is no agreed way to resolve these so as to identify a "human right" other than the process of negotiation which exists between countries in the development of conventions, declarations and treaties.

Because human rights have different contexts in different cultures, yet are at the same time universal, they are of necessity written in very general language. This allows nations to interpret those rights within their own cultural context.

An attempt to define human rights and fundamental freedoms exhaustively is bound to fail, for the respective religious, cultural and political systems of the world would attribute differing contents to the notions of freedom and dignity and would perceive at least some difference in the rights and freedoms that are conducive to their attainment. The formulation of many rights also contain limitation clauses. This was explained by one witness to the inquiry: For example, if we take article 19 and 19(3) of the International Covenant on Civil and Political Rights, we will see that the limitation on the right to free speech is cast in the following terms: it says that the right itself carries special duties and responsibilities. The covenant accepts that the right to free speech is not absolute. The covenant then says that the right may be limited where the limitation or restriction is provided by law and is necessary in a democratic society. It sets out the reasons or grounds on which the limitation will apply. The first ground is the rights and reputations of others. It goes on to list other grounds such as national security, public morals and public order. An example such as this illustrates that most rights are not absolute. Another limitation on rights is that typically one right has to be balanced against another. An example of the balancing of the right to freedom of religion as against the right for women not to be discriminated against was explored in a Committee hearing in relation to the ordination of women priests:

> Article 18.1 of the International Covenant on Civil and Political Rights protects that religion in its current form so that the current teachings, practices, observance and worship of that religion are protected by a right of religion. What is protected is the freedom to exercise one's religious beliefs. We would then be seeing a conflict with a right for all people to be treated equally. The right to equality is not an absolute right. The balance would have to be struck between two sets of competing rights and the covenants make it very clear that one person's rights may well be limited by the enjoyment and exercise of another right. In some senses, even if churches were brought within the scheme of the bill of rights, it would be to protect the churches, to protect current forms of religious organisations so that they are the beneficiaries of the rights themselves. If there is a conflict between the nature of the enjoyment of a particular religious belief and the rights of another, then the process is finding where that balance is to be struck.

While most human rights are not absolute, at least in their expression in conventions and treaties, they can be described as interdependent and indivisible. Countries that have signed the *ICCPR* for instance, have agreed to protect all of the rights contained in that instrument. This goes back to human rights being those rights which express how people's humanity should be respected: governments cannot pick and choose which aspects of being human they will respect.

A debate in the human rights area, and one which forms the term of reference of this inquiry, is to what extent "responsibilities" should be included when human rights are expressed in conventions and in local legislation. Every right implies a responsibility on the member state to honour that right. When the 1948 *Declaration* was drafted the strongest concern was to protect individual rights against the state, after the recent experience of authoritarian governments before and during the War. Governments were given responsibilities to protect their citizens' rights. However there have been arguments in recent years that part of being a citizen involves accepting responsibilities, and that over-emphasis on rights creates an attitude of avoidance of individual responsibility.

While the meaning of human rights is the subject of some debate, the sources of current human rights law is generally accepted. The original source document for current human rights is the *United Nations Declaration of Human Rights*, adopted in 1948 by the majority of the international community in response to the abuses of human rights perpetrated before and during the Second World War. It expresses basic human rights in general terms as a common standard of achievement for all peoples and all nations. These rights include the prevention of slavery and torture, the right to be treated equally regardless of race or gender, the right to own property and the right to privacy.

The covenant which has proved most influential in the development of human rights law has been the *International Covenant on Civil and Political Rights* (the *ICCPR*). This was adopted in 1966 to provide detailed explanation of the individual rights of the citizen in relation to the power of the state. Civil and political rights include the right to vote, the right to form trade unions, the right not to suffer cruel or unusual punishment and various protections to ensure a person is not subject to arbitrary arrest or detention without charge. Under Article 40 those states, which have ratified the *Convention* are given obligations to provide reports on progress in implementing the protection of these rights within their jurisdictions.

In the international community there was debate, led by developing nations, as to whether the individual rights protected by the *ICCPR* gave sufficient recognition to the problems faced in countries where inadequate food, housing and health resources were the primary consideration of its citizens. There was also a debate along ideological lines with Socialist countries arguing that rights such as those relating to employment or welfare were not properly encompassed in the *ICCPR*.

The idea of broader rights to be enjoyed by groups and individuals, drawing from the economic, social and cultural rights discussed in the 1948 Declaration, then became enshrined in the *International Covenant on Economic, Social and Cultural Rights (ICESCR)*, also adopted in 1966. The *ICESCR* provides for the right to be free from hunger, the right to education, the right to social security, the right to physical and mental health and the right of groups to enjoy their own culture and participate in cultural life. As with the *ICCPR*, those countries, that have ratified the *ICESCR* have obligations to report on progress in implementing the Convention in their jurisdictions. However, while the *ICCPR* is prescriptive in the obligations imposed, the *ICESCR's* obligations are aspirational in nature.

Apart from the *United Nations Declaration on Human Rights* and the *ICCPR* and *ICESCR* some of the conventions which have had an influence on the development of human rights are:

— The Convention on the Rights of the Child

— The International Convention on the Elimination of Racial Discrimination

— The Convention on the Elimination of all forms of Discrimination Against Women

— The Convention Relating to the Status of Refugees; and

— United Nations Draft Declaration on the rights of Indigenous Peoples.

2

Development of Human Rights

The development of the field of human rights provide hints of what a discipline of international studies that assumes that politics cannot be analyzed separate from ethics might look like. Thirty years ago, human rights were regularly studied only within the subfields of international organization and international law- and even there only as a peripheral issue. During the mid-1970s, the core of controversy, among both analysts and actors, was whether human rights was a fit subject for inclusion within a country's foreign policy. Because of its ethical dimension, many argued that human rights was an inappropriate part of international politics.

Over the past decade, however, human rights has become accepted as a standard part of both the study and the practice of international politics. It still remains a secondary interest in the foreign policy of states and most regional and international organizations. But in policy circles, the ethical dimension is increasingly treated as a fact about the character of this particular national (or international) interest. Debate is over the proper substance of international human rights policies, not whether states ought to have such policies. And human rights has become a relatively well-settled, if still peripheral, part of the discipline of international studies.

In the fifty years since it was adopted by the United Nations General Assembly, the Universal Declaration of Human Rights has been endorsed by virtually all states, arguably acquiring the status of customary international law. The International Covenant on Civil and Political Rights currently has 144 parties. The International Covenant on Economic, Social, and Cultural Rights has 141 parties. The Vienna Declaration and Programme of Action was adopted by consensus by the 171 states that participated in the 1993 World Conference on Human Rights.

Human rights have repeatedly been at the center of struggles for social justice and against political oppression across the globe. Opposition to totalitarian party-state rule in the Soviet bloc was increasingly waged through the language of human rights in the late 1970s and 1980s, spurred in significant measure by the human rights provisions of the Helsinki Final Act.

The struggle against military dictatorship in Latin America also became largely a struggle for human rights. And today in much of Africa and Asia, human rights activists are central to struggles against poverty and misrule. The language of international human rights has become almost as deeply embedded in contemporary struggles of political opposition as it is in the rhetoric of multilateral and bilateral diplomacy and the legitimating appeals of states.

Human rights are typically understood, following the manifest, literal sense of the term, as the rights that one has simply because one is human. They are universal rights: every human being has them. They are equal rights: one either is a human being (and thus has these rights equally) or not. And they are inalienable rights: one cannot stop being a human being, and thus cannot stop having these rights.

Furthermore, in the Universal Declaration, the Covenants, and the Vienna Declaration we can discern clear if thin answers to three basic conceptual and theoretical questions about human rights thus understood: what is the character of these rights (function), where do they come from (source), and what is their substance (list)? The source of internationally recognized human rights is identified as the inherent (moral) nature of the human person. Article 1 of the Universal Declaration begins "All human beings are born free and equal in dignity and rights." Both Covenants assert that "these rights derive from the inherent dignity of the human person." The Vienna Declaration uses almost the same language: "all human rights derive from the dignity and worth inherent in the human person."

Every person, simply as a human being, is entitled to enjoy her human rights. "Everyone has the right ..." "No one shall be ..." "Every human being has ..." Individuals are properly subject to a great array of social and political obligations. Human rights, however, specify an inalienable set of goods, services, and opportunities that the state and society are, in ordinary circumstances, required to respect or provide to those under their jurisdiction. By thus restricting the legitimate range of state action, internationally recognized human rights function as a standard of political legitimacy, and thus as a ground for struggles against misrule and injustice.

The Universal Declaration proclaims itself "a common standard of achievement for all peoples and all nations." The Vienna Declaration is unusually forthright, claiming in its first operative paragraph protecting and promotion human rights "is the first responsibility of Governments."

Other systems for regulating relations between individuals, states, and society have been the norm throughout most of history, in all regions of the world. Tradition, gender, age, birth, divine right, charisma, ethnicity, superior culture, and religion have been some of the more prominent grounds for establishing a just title to rule. Contemporary international society, however, has endorsed human rights in the strongest possible terms.

The Universal Declaration and the Covenants are primarily lists of human rights. These rights are seen, in the language of the Vienna Declaration, as "universal, indivisible and interdependent and interrelated. ... it is the duty of States, regardless of their political, economic and cultural systems, to promote and protect all human rights and fundamental freedoms." Thus the motto of the office of the High Commissioner for Human Rights for 1998, the fiftieth anniversary of the Universal Declaration, was "All human rights for all." The duties correlative to internationally recognized human rights, however, fall largely on states.

Although human rights are held by every person, they target the state of which one is a national.

International human rights treaties create obligations for states to respect, protect, and implement the rights of their own citizens. They do not provide international legal justification for coercive action to implement or protect the rights of foreigners abroad. They thus leave largely untouched the central international legal principle of non-intervention. Although human rights norms have been internationalized, their implementation remains largely national. Coercive uses of force, and thus international enforcement in a strong sense of that term, remain largely prohibited.

It is conventional to distinguish deontological (duty-based) theories, such as Kant's categorical imperative, from teleological (ends-, goals-, or consequence-based) theories, such as Bentham's utilitarianism. Such theories posit radically different relationships between the right and the good. Right is the moral primitive for deontological theories. We are required to do what is right (follow our duty), period, independent of the effects, for good or bad, produced by our actions. "Thou shalt not ..." The moral primitive in teleological theories, by contrast, is the good. Duty depends on the consequences of our actions. We are morally required to, within the limits of our skill and resources, increase human happiness or reduce human suffering. This common classification of moral theories, however, tells us little about human rights, which have played a vanishingly small part in the history of (Western) moral theory, even during the modern era. For example, rights are hardly mentioned in Kant's *Grounding for the Metaphysics of Morals*.

For utilitarians, rights are only second order rules that save us the (often considerable) task of calculating utilities in particular cases. Although Ronald Dworkin has talked about rights-based moral theories, such a category has historically been largely an empty one. Human rights logically may be, but in fact rarely have been, taken to be a moral primitive. They can, however, be relatively easily derived from many moral theories. Human rights might, for example, be seen as encoded in natural law. Teleological theories might ground a system of rights in their tendency to further human good or flourishing. Nonetheless, one of the most striking theoretical features of human rights is their loose connection to modern moral theories.

When we turn to political theory, however, (human) rights often become central. This is perhaps most striking in Kant's "Theory and Practice." Part I, which deals with individual morality, sketches a radically egalitarian deontological ethic that makes no significant reference to rights. But in Part II, which treats what Kant calls "political right," rights (entitlements) become central. In fact, Kant's contractarian political theory is centered on the rights we have as human beings, as subjects, and as citizens. As this example suggests, human rights are at the heart-in fact a defining feature-of contractarian political theories.

Other political theories may endorse a human rights standard of political legitimacy by other routes. One might even argue that the loose and weak link between human rights and leading moral theories is an attraction rather than a drawback, allowing for a considerable degree of political consensus despite otherwise important moral divergence. Although incompatible with virtually all inegalitarian theories, human rights, by remaining open to many egalitarian moral and political theories, may allow us to handle certain questions of political justice and right while circumventing difficult and often acrimonious disputes over moral foundations. This is particularly attractive in a "postmodern" world skeptical of the possibility of finding logically unassailable foundations. Political theorists have increasingly turned their attention to notions such as deliberative consensus-for example, in the recent work of both John Rawls and Jurgen Habermas and recognition. Human rights may provide a focal point for forging such a consensus or for negotiating mutual recognition. Certainly there is no other substantive ideal that has come even close to such widespread international endorsement by both governments and movements of political opposition across the globe.

The "universality" of human rights is a normative claim about the proper way to organize social and political relations in the contemporary world, not an historical or anthropological fact. All societies have conceptions of personal dignity, ideal visions of the life-or more often, lives-fit for (different groups of) human beings. All cultures and societies appeal to social values such as equity, fairness, compassion, and respect for one's fellows. Very few, however, have defined one's fellows as all members of the species homo sapiens or have sought to realize these values through equal and inalienable universal rights held by every citizen against society. That is the perspective, however, that has been adopted by contemporary international society.We are most immediately familiar with the regulative aspects of human rights norms: "No one shall be subjected to torture or to cruel, inhuman or degrading treatment or punishment;" "All are equal before the law and are entitled without any discrimination to equal protection of the law;" "Everyone has the right to work, to free choice of employment, to just and favorable conditions of work and to protection against unemployment." No less importantly, however, human rights norms constitute individuals as a particular kind of political subject-free and equal rights-bearing citizens-and define the requirements and limits of legitimate government.

Human beings are, of course, members of social groups and occupants of social roles. "Individuals" are also members of families and communities, workers, church-goers, citizens, and occupants of numerous other social roles. Nonetheless, a human rights conception of politics insists that essential to their dignity, and to a life worthy of a human being, is the simple fact that they are distinct and separate individual human beings. These individuals are in the first instance equal. But this core commitment to equality leads "naturally" to an emphasis on autonomy. Equal individuals have no right to force on one another ideas of what is right and proper. More precisely, they have no right to force on others obligations that treat them as less than equal moral agents. Human rights link equality and autonomy through the notion of (individual and collective) self-determination, an ideal with extremely wide and deep political resonance.

Without implying complete license, human rights limit what society may legitimately prohibit or require of its members. Equal and autonomous rights-bearing individuals are entitled to make fundamental choices about what constitutes the good life (for them) and with whom they associate and how. Each individual thus must be treated by the state with equal concern and respect. A list of (human and legal) rights reflects a particular understanding of the meaning of equal concern and respect, based on a substantive conception of human dignity or the conditions required to permit human flourishing. But human rights also promise to (re)shape political and social relations so that this moral vision will be realized. Equal, inalienable rights held by all against state and society provide a mechanism for realizing such a world of equal and autonomous human beings. The effective implementation of the specified rights will produce the envisioned person/life (assuming a certain coherence and practicality in that vision). Human rights thus are simultaneously a "utopian" vision and a set of institutions-equal and inalienable rights-for realizing at least an approximation of that vision.

As a political theory, human rights focus on relations between subjects and rulers-or, in the language of egalitarian politics, citizens and their governments. We can trace a progression over the past century and a quarter through four (overlapping) conceptions of international political legitimacy.

1) "Classical" political realists and legal positivists granted full membership in international society to organized political groups (states) with the capacity to maintain their political autonomy and control their own territory and a willingness to enter into international obligations and participate in established practices of diplomacy This "Hobbesian" vision presents international relations as a state of war, and international recognition as properly determined by the facts of control over people and territory. National legitimacy is left as a matter of sovereign prerogative.

2) The late nineteenth and early twentieth century "standard of civilization" added the requirements of respect for the laws of war and certain rights of

(Western) aliens, as well as the prohibition of shockingly "uncivilized" practices such as slavery, polygamy, and "barbaric" penal practices. These minimal international standards of national political legitimacy reflect a more "Burkean" conception of politics that sees some peoples as having greater virtue than others, and thus entitled to more rights and a greater say in politics. It rejects Hobbes' egalitarian universalism, minimalist as it might be, in favor of an inegalitarian, "communitarian" conception of social and political development.

3) The anti-colonial idea of "self-determination"- understood in Cold War era practice as decolonization of Western overseas holdings and punctilious respect for the legal principles of sovereign equality and nonintervention-in effect extended to all states the formal rights enjoyed by the nineteenth century "Powers." The conception of international legitimacy, however, remained largely Hobbesian: the right to life (sovereignty and territorial integrity) was recognized, but not much else. Furthermore, the international community largely refused to inquire into questions of national legitimacy, which were seen as a matter of self-determination.

4) Human rights has become the dominant conception of political legitimacy over the past two decades. Like the classical standard of civilization, it is a standard of national as well as international legitimacy. But it is an egalitarian standard. And its substantive requirements are quite extensive. Legitimacy is thus measured in terms of the interests of people as well as those of states. In fact, the interests of the people, and any plausible conception of human dignity, are

seen to require the harnessing of the immense power and reach of the modern state.

The human rights strategy of state control has had two principal dimensions. Negatively, human rights prohibit a wide range of state interferences in the personal, social, and political lives of citizens, acting both individually and collectively. No less important, however, is the positive empowerment of the people, who are sees as above and in control of their government. Political authority is vested in a free citizenry endowed with extensive rights of political participation (universal suffrage, freedom of association, free speech, etc.). And by requiring the people, through the state, to provide certain goods, services, and opportunities (as specified in the reigning list of human rights), the regulation of economic markets is brought centrally within the purview of the state. The state thus is seen not simply as a potential threat to human dignity but not less importantly as the central institution with the capacity to implement internationally recognized civil, political, economic, and social human rights. "Failed states" such as Somalia suggests that one of the few things as frightening as an efficiently repressive state is no state at all.

Human rights, in addition to seeking to prevent certain state-based wrongs, require the state to provide certain goods, services, and opportunities and to protect individuals and families from market-based suffering. This positive role of the state is as central for civil and political rights as for economic and social rights. Effective implementation of the right to nondiscrimination, for example, often requires extensive positive actions. Even procedural rights such as due process entail considerable positive endeavors by police, courts, and administrative agencies. The state must not merely refrain from certain harmful actions but create a social and political environment that fosters the development of active, engaged, autonomous citizens. Rights-bearing individuals alone cannot effectively implement their rights or make for themselves a life worthy of human beings. Hobbes put the point most forcefully in arguing that in a pre-social state of nature, life would be "solitary, poor, nasty, brutish, and short." Human rights require social provision. And the substance of contemporary international human rights norms emphasizes collective, public activity as essential to a life of human dignity. The Universal Declaration of Human Rights and the International Human Rights Covenants codify an evolved shared understanding of the principal systematic public threats to human dignity in the contemporary world and the social and political practices necessary to counter them. To oversimplify only slightly, they set out as a hegemonic political model something very much like the liberal democratic welfare state, in which all adult nationals are incorporated as full legal and political equals entitled to an extensive array of social welfare services, social and economic opportunities, and civil and political liberties.

However attractive one find the human rights vision of political dignity and legitimacy, the close tie to the state is problematic. The dominant contemporary conception of human rights mixes a cosmopolitan, universalistic vision of the source and subjects of human rights with a particularistic, nationalist vision of their implementation. This rather awkward compromise is most often assumed rather than justified. Practically, it reflects the continuing dominance of the sovereign state, which remains the only agent widely capable of delivering the goods, services, and opportunities specified by international human rights norms. But can this political fact be morally justified? Consider Article 28 of the Universal Declaration: "Everyone is entitled to a social and international order in which the rights and freedoms set forth in this Declaration can be fully realized." Is a system of sovereign, territorial states such an order? If so, is it the best such order? If not, is there a better practical alternative? If, in contractarian terms, we can see the state as the free choice of self-determining individuals and communities, then a world of sovereign territorial states may satisfy the demands of Article 28.

But even setting aside severely repressive regimes that cannot plausibly be imagined to reflect either the autonomous will of the people or the requirements of internationally recognized human rights, this privileging of the state is problematic. We should remain open to the possibility of right-holders choosing to exercise their rights collectively in communities smaller or larger than states. Consider, for example, contemporary Europe, in which we see strong pressures to both regional integration and sub-national devolution of power.

Individuals increasingly act within multiple political communities that reflect cross-cutting loyalties and identities, in contrast to the totalizing centralization of political power and identity in the nationalist state. In Belgium, Spain, and to a somewhat lesser extent Britain, we see fragmenting national identities and the emergence of non-state political communities that might suggest a more diverse and pluralistic conception of social actors with human rights obligations. If recent talk about transnational or global civil society is more than metaphorical or prescriptive, this is another possibility worth taking seriously. In any case, it would be dangerous to treat the currently dominant statist conception of political community uncritically as a fixed feature. Individual right-holders in principle have many more options within which they may choose to interact and seek to realize their rights.

Recent efforts to establish international responsibility for genocide and related gross and systematic violations of internationally recognized human rights present a direct if implicit challenge to the statism of the Universal Declaration and the Covenants. Under realist/positivist, standard of civilization, and self-determination conceptions of international legitimacy, how a state treats its own citizens within its own territory was largely unregulated by international standards International responsibility for national human rights practices therefore was virtually nil.

Human rights violators were not legally accountable and international actors had no right to intervene even in response to the most gruesome violations. During the Cold War, most former dictators could expect, at worst, a comfortable retirement abroad in pleasant if somewhat isolated circumstances. Even genocide was met by expressions of shock and outrage coupled with inaction against the perpetrators. This is no longer the case. Ad hoc tribunals for the former Yugoslavia and Rwanda and the new International Criminal Court have established individual responsibility for genocide and crimes against humanity.

Violators are seen as having international human rights obligations to international society, in addition to their direct and primary obligation to the right-holders under their jurisdiction. In addition, multilateral field operations in places such as Somalia, Cambodia, Bosnia,

Rwanda, and Kosovo suggest a different, but no less important, sort of international responsibility. These operations involve international society asserting a right to provide limited redress to victims, who are no longer left to the mercies of a purely national system of implementing internationally recognized human rights. In certain cases, international community will act on their behalf. Such a limited doctrine of humanitarian intervention can be seen as an unfolding of the self-determination justification for sovereignty noted above. No free people could be imagined to choose for themselves treatment such as that suffered by, for example, Muslims and Croats in Bosnia or Serbs in Croatia following the breakup of Yugoslavia. International intervention is justified to restore the conditions under which self-determination is possible. But once a plausible argument of self-determination can be advanced, the obligation of non-intervention again takes priority.

Rights are enjoyed within nested political communities. And this nesting challenges the previously accepted exclusive claims of sovereign territorial states. Sovereign states and ruling governments are coming to be seen to have international human rights obligations not just to their own nationals but also to the international community. And these international responses have often been in situations where the victims were singled out in significant measure on the basis of their membership in an ethnic or other subnational community. In thus asserting both obligations to the international community and rights of subnational communities to a protected sphere of difference, the awkward compromise between statist and cosmopolitan conceptions of community would seem to be shifting, subtly yet significantly, against the state. We should not over-estimate the scope of these (undoubtedly important) changes.

Humanitarian intervention remains a right rather than an obligation. Should international society fail to act forcefully, victims have no established recourse. And as Kosovo indicates, the nature and authority of the relevant "higher" community many not be clear or endorsed by anything close to the full range of interested and involved international actors. Furthermore, we should not assume an inevitable, or even likely, spillover from cases of genocide and crimes against humanity to more "ordinary" human rights violations.

Coercive international enforcement of internationally recognized human rights remains rare and largely restricted to broader peace and security operations. Even severe violations in "ordinary" situations usually are not seen to authorize coercive international enforcement. Nonetheless, we do seem to be witnessing modest but important changes in dominant views of the obligations correlative to internationally recognized human rights. The international community, in at least some limited circumstances, may assert priority over states to assure the protection of internationally recognized human rights. And many of the leading cases involve the international community acting to protect subnational communities from a government that punishes them for their difference.

The simple state-citizen model of politics implicit in the Universal Declaration is at least fraying on the edges. States are coming to be seen as having human rights obligations to other states or the international community, as well as their own citizens. In at least these limited cases, the political universality of human rights is significantly extended. Furthermore, human rights link individuals to both national and international communities, at least partially re-opening questions of national and international political legitimacy and the proper relation between individuals, seen as bearers of internationally recognized human rights, and the various communities in which they carry out their lives.

The idea that certain practices simply cannot be justified raises the issue of cultural relativism. An extensive literature in the 1970s and 1980s addressed the claim that there are radically different but entirely defensible regional, cultural, political, or religious conceptions of human rights-for example, African, Islamic, Western, Socialist, and Third World conceptions. In the 1990s, a parallel argument about "Asian values" has received considerable attention.

The idea of human rights appeals to values and social practices that transcend cultural and political differences-however important those difference might be in other contexts. Any interesting sense of the adjective "human" requires that these rights be in some sense universal. And the standard language of universal human rights clearly reflects such an understanding. The challenge of cultural relativism thus addresses (a) the substantive extent of these (universal) rights and (b) their force relative to competing cultural and political claims. If there are few universal rights and if the competing claims of society regularly take priority over even those rights, then the resulting vision of human rights is extremely relativist. Conversely, an extensive list of rights that usually take priority over competing social claims yields a relatively universalist vision of human rights.

Real disputes about the substance of internationally recognized human rights certainly do exist. For example, the right to property appears in the Universal Declaration, was not included in the Covenants, but has made a considerable comeback in the 1990s. The international legal prohibition of "hate speech" is inconsistent with American constitutional law. Many Muslims reject the right to change one's religion (if it is Islam) or to have no religion at all.. Nonetheless, when we consider the extent of the list of rights in the Universal Declaration and the Covenants and the degree of cultural and political diversity in the world, there is a remarkable degree of consensus about the list of internationally recognized human rights. Few major states or social groups categorically reject more than a few of the rights in the Universal Declaration. Debate instead usually focuses on the implications of particular rights, priorities among them, and conflicts between human rights and other social and political values and concerns.

At its deepest level, the debate between relativism and universalism concerns our conception of human beings. Do we see them principally through the lens of what they share or how they differ? We might want to say that the issue is whether we think of people primarily as human beings or as social beings. But given the obvious fact that human beings live human lives only within rich and complex social settings, a better way to pose the question is "Do we see our social life more as an expression of a common humanity or a series of often very different yet internally authoritative answers to the question of what it means to be human?" If the universality of human rights is a prescriptive claim about the proper way to organize society and if human rights are constitutive norms, then the resulting account of human rights must be in some important sense relativist. Most societies have rejected these norms and have constituted social, political, and moral actors with identities very different from that of equal citizens with extensive rights against society. Rather than transcendent values, the "grounds" or "foundations" of human rights are social acceptance in "our" world today. Their justification is ultimately functional: we accept human rights because of the social, political, and moral consequences of acting as required to realize these rights.

The inherent human dignity on which human rights rest is a social project, not a fact of nature or reason. Within this general theoretical relativism, however, a strong case can be made for the relative universality of internationally recognized human rights. Human rights represent our best effort to respond to the standard threats to human dignity posed by modern markets and modern states-which, in the contemporary world, have penetrated almost all of the globe. In addition, the list of internationally recognized human rights reflects a relatively highly evolved, and still changing, conception of the minimum conditions for a life of dignity. Consider the case of economic and social rights.

The "classic" Lockean list includes only the right to property. But we came to learn that this provided minimum economic dignity only for a small segment of society. And after much struggle by the excluded masses, dominant conceptions of economic and social rights changed dramatically. To take a very different example, in the contemporary world, where health is seen less as a matter of fortune and more as a matter for social provision, a right to health care has become central to our conception of a life of dignity-at least in countries other than the United States. Given that it is relatively uncontroversial to say that the threats of states and markets are indeed (relatively) universal, the heart of the challenge of cultural relativism becomes a claim that in the contemporary world there is not considerable cross-cultural convergence on the underlying conception of human dignity expressed in the Universal Declaration.

Universality of the Universal Declaration

Non-western societies give more emphasis to the group whereas western societies give more emphasis to the individual. There is a lot of (politically dangerous) caricature here. For the sake of argument, however, let us accept this claim. What does it imply as a challenge to the universality of the Universal Declaration? Not much. Articles 2 and 7, which requires non-discrimination and equality before the law, are usually stressed at least as much by Third World as western governments and activists. The rights to life, liberty, security of the person, legal recognition, and protection against slavery and torture (Articles 3-6) have as wide an applicability in nonwestern as in western societies in the contemporary world. Much the same is true of legal rights to remedy, the presumption of innocence, and protection against arbitrary arrest or detention. Article 12's insistence that "No one shall be subjected to arbitrary interference with his privacy, family, home or correspondence, nor to attacks upon his honour and reputation" has unusually wide cross-cultural resonance. Even some "individualistic" civil and political rights have surprisingly wide appeal. Consider Articles 18-21. "Everyone has the right to freedom of thought, conscience and religion." "Everyone has the right to freedom of opinion and expression." "Everyone has the right to freedom of peaceful assembly and association." "Everyone has the right to take part in the government of his country, directly or through freely chosen representatives." Even most governments that in practice systematically deny these rights rarely admit that that is what they are doing. Certain rights are more genuinely problematic. Consider, for example, Article 16.

1. Men and women of full age, without any limitation due to race, nationality or religion, have the right to marry and to found a family. They are entitled to equal rights as to marriage, during marriage and at its dissolution.

2. Marriage shall be entered into only with the free and full consent of the intending spouses.

This does indeed seem to express a particular "modern" "western" conception of marriage. But if we exercise a modest degree of interpretative liberty with the phrase "free and full consent of the intending spouses," considerable accommodation to "traditional" conceptions of the family and marriage are possible. In particular, so long as intending spouses are legally free to enter into a marriage or not, and are able to receive legal protection if they decide not to accept arranged marriages, the social pressures to accommodate broader family interests-which, of course, also exist in parts of many western societies as well-usually will be acceptable. Furthermore, many of the group-oriented cultural differences to which relativists appeal can be accommodated by the way that right-holders exercise their rights. For example, if Asians are more deferential, they will choose to exercise their civil liberties in more deferential ways than, say,

Americans do. Those who are excessively aggressive or individualistic in the expression of their views are likely to have less attractive employment prospects and are unlikely to be elected to political office. They may even be shunned by wide segments of society.

Human rights do not prohibit such social sanctions for behavior that fails to conform to social norms. They only require that the state not punish or discriminate against those with unpopular views or abrasive ways of expressing them. But although societies do have considerable latitude in shaping their implementation of such rights, there are limits. The state may not incarcerate, harass, or deny otherwise available benefits or services to individuals simply because they hold or publicly express unpopular, or even offensive, religious or political beliefs. Female children may not be treated as chattel, to be disposed of in marriage at the discretion of their family.

The claim of the Universal Declaration is that even where such practices have deep cultural roots as they did in the West just a hundred years ago-they can no longer be justified. For slavery, torture, the denial of legal personality, or the denial of food, such a claim is relatively unproblematic. Many societies have practiced slavery. That simply does not justify it today-so long as we accept the basic notion that all human beings are entitled to certain basic goods, services, and opportunities. Torture has been a common practice in many societies. It simply is no longer acceptable, given the reigning conception of the right to personal security and bodily integrity.

Many societies have allowed large numbers of people to starve in the face of natural or social disasters.

Almost nowhere is this accepted today. Much the same is true of just about all the rights in the Universal Declaration. They are in fact widely endorsed, by both governments and citizens. And where they are not, a very heavy burden of proof lies on those who would claim that the right ought not to apply in their society. Occasionally, this may lead to a moral impasse. Perhaps the clearest examples involve religious fundamentalist regimes such as the Taliban in Afghanistan and the clerical governments that have ruled Iran for the past two decades. These governments do explicitly claim that they recognize human rights only to the extent that they are already incorporated within divine revelation or established religious law and tradition. The fact that they are internationally recognized human rights is essentially irrelevant in the eyes of these regimes. Where there is conformity with international human rights norms, that is purely a matter of coincidence. We are significantly constrained by the overarching commitment to individual autonomy and collective self-determination. If people choose to make for themselves a life that rejects our vision of the good life, that is, within certain limits, their choice. The question then becomes determining whether indeed they have made that choice or had it imposed upon them.

Often the "cultural" differences in question are relatively recent creations, or even the creations of "outside" forces-such as the creation of Hutu and Tutsi ethnicities by Belgian colonial officials. More often than not, they are political rather than cultural differences, involving at best a highly selective appropriation of local traditions. For example, revolutionary governments that engage in the massive repression of dissent usually have a hard time justifying their behavior by truly cultural arguments. China presents a particularly striking example of misplaced "cultural relativist" arguments: a communist party state dictatorship fully in control of the coercive apparatus of a modern state and army and actively hostile to most elements of traditional Chinese culture simply cannot plausibly be seen as an expression of "Chinese culture," however we might want to understand that term. Even when political differences do have a deep "cultural" basis, it is often hijacked by political interests. If we are to take cultural relativism seriously as an ethical position, we must abandon the unthinking statism that accepts whatever a government does as the expression of the will of its people. We must inquire, as a matter of fact, whether the practices in question have been chosen by or imposed upon a people. If the latter, there may be legal, political, or practical reasons not to intervene. But there is no moral reason to stand by idly.

Even the free choices of a people are subject to limits. If a majority chooses to massacre, enslave, or systematically subordinate a minority through force, outsiders face a choice of which side to support. Only if we believe that all values are simply a matter of majority choice are we bound to choose a repressive majority-and even that is not clear if an international majority has condemned such practices.

Conversely, there are a variety of good reasons, including universal human rights, for outsiders to choose to aid the minority. What form that aid should take is often a difficult question, as NATO's efforts in Kosovo vividly illustrate. When the violations of international human rights norms are less systematic or substantially less brutal, determining an appropriate international response is even more difficult. Nonetheless, outsiders are not ethically obliged to abandon foreigners to the mercies of their governments or societies. States or societies that wish to make a plausible ethical appeal to an international obligation of non-intervention must be able to point to something more than their control over their territory by force. An argument that we have done it this way for a long time, or that some segment of the population wishes to do it this way now, simply is not persuasive. Those who wish to have their rights to sovereignty and self-determination respected can, in at least some cases, be plausibly required to respect the self-determination and basic human rights of those over whom they rule. And even if considerations of law or politics lead outsiders not to intervene with force, they have every right to condemn systematic violations of internationally recognized human rights and to use other means of foreign policy to encourage guilty governments to change their practices.

In practice, relativist arguments have had significant ethical force in few cases where there has been a strong ethical inclination to intervene on behalf of victims of gross human rights violations. Even if it is the way of Serbs to massacre Muslims in Bosnia and Kosovo, that is no reason for non-Serbs to accept that way. Much the same is true of Sudanese Muslims massacring non-Muslims in the south of their country, or governments in Guatemala and Paraguay massacring their native peoples, or Burma's government expelling a quarter million Burmese Muslims, or Somali clan leaders fighting one another and leaving hundreds of thousands to die of starvation. When it comes to cases such as the Khmer Rouge in Cambodia, where traditional culture was an explicit target of repression, arguments of cultural relativism becomes a cruel joke. Much the same is true today of North Korea or Sierra Leone, where barbarism seems to have replaced any plausible conception of culture. And in countless other cases- e.g., China, Cuba, Iraq, Burma, and Afghanistan to take some of the more extreme cases; or, less extremely, Indonesia, Cambodia, and Pakistan-where people are daily being forced to be what their government insists their cultural or political destiny commands them to be, the joke is only somewhat less cruel. Perhaps the strongest evidence in support of the relative universality of internationally recognized human rights is the fact that the protections provided by internationally recognized human rights seem to be widely desired by most people in most parts of the world.

When allowed a choice, most people in all regions of the world have chosen human rights. And most regimes that systematically reject extensive portions of the Universal Declaration retain power only through systematic repression-which clearly evidences the regime's lack of legitimacy in the eyes of its own people. If we are not to treat human beings as objects at the mercy of their government or society, some substantial appeal to "higher" values is required. Such appeals are undoubtedly morally problematic. But strong cultural relativism faces even more severe moral problems. And when the universalistic appeal is to international human rights norms, which have been remarkably widely endorsed by both states and citizens more or less across the globe, a position of relative universalism seems by far the least problematic course.

The post-Cold War world has also seen growing international endorsement of democracy as a form of political rule and markets as the basis of economic organization. The mutually reinforcing linkages between human rights, democracy, and markets are well known and regularly noted. In the United States, and in certain political circles in Britain and other countries, it has even become common to speak of the ideal regime type as "market democracies."

Human Rights and Democracy

Democracy is based on the freely expressed will of the people to determine their own political, economic, social and cultural systems and their full participation in all aspects of their lives." This statement from the Vienna Declaration, like all plausible definitions, is rooted in the etymology of the term, the Greek demokratia, literally, rule or power (kratos) of the people (demos). Thus David Held begins Models of Democracy, an often cited recent scholarly work, by defining democracy as a form of government in which, in contradistinction to monarchies and aristocracies, the people rule.

Of particular salience are the continuing debates over balancing democratic procedures (government by the people, in Jefferson's famous formula) with "substantive" democracy (government for the people). As a result, discussions of democracy as a political ideal usually shift their attention fairly rapidly to the adjectives-substantive, procedural, electoral, direct, representative, liberal, guided, people's-rather than the noun democracy. Rule of the people and respect for human rights often point in very different directions as a result of their very different visions of the relationship between society and its individual members. Democracy in this root sense aims to empower the people, to assure that they, rather than some other group in society, rule.

But it requires little of the sovereign people, who, as the Vienna Declaration put it, are free "to determine their own political, economic, social and cultural systems." Only if a sovereign people wills respect for human rights, and thus constrains its own interests and actions, will democracy contribute to realizing human rights. In practice, however, the will of the people, no matter how it is ascertained, often diverges from the rights of individual citizens. Human rights, by contrast, aim to empower individuals, thus limiting rather than empowering the sovereign people and their government. By requiring that every person receive certain goods, services, and opportunities, the acceptable range of political, economic, social, and cultural systems and practices is severely restricted. Beyond who ought to rule-which is indeed given a democratic answer-human rights are concerned with what rulers do, with how the people rules.

Human rights thus are in an important sense profoundly anti-democratic. Their aim is to frustrate the will of the people when it diverges from the requirements of human rights. The American system of constitutional review by an "undemocratic," even "anti-democratic," Supreme Court provides a good example. One of its central purposes to assure that the people, through their elected representatives, do not exercise their sovereignty in ways that violate basic rights. Governments in Britain, France, India, Japan, Costa Rica, South Africa, and the U.S. are indeed democratic. But what makes them truly attractive is the fact that they are what students of comparative politics typically call liberal democracies, a very specific kind of (democratic) government in which the morally and politically prior rights of citizens (and the requirement of the rule of law) limit the range of democratic decision-making. Democracy and human rights are mutually reinforcing in contemporary liberal democracies only because of a particular resolution of the competing claims of democracy and human rights that gives priority to human rights.

The democratic logic of popular rule operates only within the constraints set by individual human rights. The adjective "liberal" rather than the noun "democracy" does most of the human rights work. The struggle for liberal democracy is a struggle for human rights- but only because human rights have been built into the definition through the adjective. These vital distinctions have been obscured in many discussions of the late Cold War and early post-Cold War spread of (largely electoral) democracy, especially in Latin America and Eastern Europe. These "democratic revolutions" have undoubtedly benefited human rights.

But even where anti-democratic forces have not reasserted themselves, many of these countries continue to systematically violate numerous internationally recognized human rights. Those not part of the majority- or whatever group exercises the power of the people- need the protection of human rights against the interests and will of "the people." This is not a matter of "immature" (merely electoral) versus "mature" (liberal) democracies.

Liberal democracy is tempered or constrained, not matured (fully developed), electoral democracy. Similar difficulties beset efforts to talk about liberal democracy as thick, full, or robust, in contrast to a thin electoral democracy. The differences are qualitative, not quantitative. Rather than completing or realizing the full logic of popular rule, liberal democracy puts popular rule in its "proper" place, subordinate to human rights in most cases of conflict. Human rights draw our attention to the fact that all individuals, simply as human beings, have powerful claims against society that typically override the preferences of even the vast majority. Democracy, by contrast, is a fundamentally collectivist or "communitarian" political logic. Its concern is not to protect individual rights, but to assure popular control of government. These very different political logics can be combined in a variety of ways. Only when human rights set the limits of democratic governance are democratic governments likely to be rights-protective regimes.

Development and Human Rights

Definitions of development are almost as diverse as, and perhaps even more contentious than, definitions of democracy. As in the case of democracy, human rights and development can be made compatible. But "development," in standard, plausible, and even attractive sense of that term, can be pursued in ways that undermine internationally recognized human rights. Not all good things necessarily go together. Consider the currently popular notion of "sustainable human development."

As defined by the United Nations Development Programme (UNDP), it includes empowerment, cooperation, equity, sustainability, and security. It may be true that "human rights and sustainable human development are inextricably linked" but only because human rights, along with democracy, peace, and justice, have been thus defined as subsets of development. Even if we agree that "true" development is "sustainable human development," we still face the problem that economic development can, and regularly is, pursued in ways that do not aim to realize internationally recognized human rights. This is particularly true when economic development is understood as it typically is today-as at it core a matter of fostering market-based systems ,of production and exchange.

Markets are social institutions designed to produce economic efficiency. Smoothly functioning market systems of production and distribution characteristically produce a greater output of goods and services with a given quantity of resources than alternative schemes. There is thus an almost tautological relationship between markets and rapid growth- which does seem to be substantively linked to realizing economic and social rights. Countries such as Cuba and Sri Lanka, which achieved short- and medium-run success but long-run failure under development plans that emphasized state-based (re-)distribution over market-based growth, suggest that a considerable degree of economic efficiency (and thus market mechanisms) is necessary for sustainable progress in implementing economic and social rights. Nonetheless, like (pure) democracy, (free) markets are justified by arguments of collective good and aggregate benefit, not individual rights (other than, perhaps, the right to economic accumulation).

Markets foster efficiency, not social equity or the enjoyment of individual rights for all. Rather than ensure that every person is treated with concern and respect, markets systematically deprive some individuals to achieve the collective benefits of efficiency. Markets distribute growth without regard for individual needs and rights (other than property rights) necessarily and by design. Market distributions are based on contribution to economic value added, which varies sharply and systematically across social groups (as well as between individuals). The poor tend to be "less efficient;" as a class, they have fewer of the skills valued highly by markets. Therefore, they are systematically disadvantaged. And their plight is exacerbated when economic and political disadvantage interact in a vicious rights-abusive cycle.Market advocates typically argue that in return for such short-run disadvantages for the few, everyone benefits from the greater supply of goods and services made available through growth. "Everyone," however, does not mean each (every) person. The referent instead is the average "individual," an abstract collective entity. And even "he" is assured significant gain only in the future. In the here and now, and well into the future, many real, flesh and blood, human beings and families suffer.

Efficient markets improve the lot of some-ideally the many- only at the (relative and perhaps even absolute) cost of suffering by others. That suffering is concentrated among society's most vulnerable elements. Even worse, because markets distribute the benefits of growth without regard to short-term deprivations, those who suffer "adjustment costs"-lost jobs, higher food prices, inferior health care or education-acquire no special claim to a share of the collective benefits that efficient markets produce. One's "fair share" is a function solely of efficiency, of monetary value added.

The human value of suffering, the human costs of deprivation, and the claims they justify, are excluded from the accounting of markets. The trick, as in the case of democracy, is to tame markets by allowing them to operate only within the constraints of the "higher" demands of internationally recognized human rights. In the liberal democracies of the Western world, the mechanism for achieving this has been the welfare state.All existing liberal democracies compensate those who fare less well in the market through the welfare state. Individuals who are harmed by the operation of social institutions that benefit the whole-markets and private property rights-are recognized to have a right to a fair share of the social product their participation has helped to produce. The collectivity that benefits in the aggregate has an obligation to look after individual members who are disadvantaged in or harmed by markets.

The welfare state guarantees all individuals certain economic and social goods, services, and opportunities irrespective of the market value of their labor. Assuaging short-term suffering and assuring long-term recompense are the work of the state, not the market. These are matters of justice, rights, and obligations, not efficiency. They raise issues of individual rights. Markets simply cannot address them because they are not designed to. Free markets are an economic analog to a political system of majority rule without minority rights. The welfare state, from this perspective, is a device to assure that a minority that is disadvantaged in or deprived by markets is treated with minimum economic concern and respect. And because this minority is shifting and indeterminate-much like the minority that would engage in unpopular political speech or be subject to arbitrary arrest-these "minority rights" are actually individual rights for all.

Rights-protective regimes will pursue economic development. But development is desirable as much for the resources it makes available to provide economic and social rights for members of disadvantaged groups as for the intrinsic values of the goods produced. Rights-protective regimes will also be democratic. They are desirable, however, not primarily because they empower the people, but because we think that we have good reason to believe that empowering the people is the best political mechanism we have yet devised to secure all human rights for all.

Human Rights, Law and Power

Human rights are rooted in justice, first and foremost. Yet, the global venture for the protection of human dignity is shaped in modern universalistic law, with bureaucratic mechanisms of standard-setting, monitoring and procedures to enforce compliance. Consequently, the whole project has certain traits of a functional system, and it is precisely in its fundamental link to morality that the human rights system needs constant renurturing from a lifeworld perspective. The tendency to abuse power is as old as human history. Therefore the use of power should always be tied to certain norms. Where such norms express legal protection of the fundamental freedoms and basic entitlements of each and every human being, we speak of 'human rights'. Since here human dignity itself is at stake, claims based on these rights should normally trump other types of claims, both private and public.

However, the global endeavour for the realization of human rights suffers from a huge deficit that is all too often submerged in the general euphoria of human rights declarations, conferences, committee meetings and workshops. Watch, for example, the still so difficult struggle against impunity of state-related perpetrators of violations of civil and political rights; look at the apparent lack of protection offered to minorities; consider the continued barrier of the public -private divide and its paralysing effects on the struggle against domestic violence; note the non-fulfilment of economic, social and cultural rights (ESCR) in a world in which so many people's basic needs remain denied. That fundamental weakness in human rights concerns their relation to social reality: declared rights, all too often, at the beginning of what are bound to be long and enduring struggles for implementation rather than acquired rights in the sense of formal legal protection of freedoms and titles that had already acquired societal recognition as sources of entitlements.

The purpose of rights, as interests protected by law, is to put conflicts of interests in a normative setting and thus to prevent their manifestation as pure power struggles. But although rights are abstract acknowledgements of claims in the sense of a general commitment to offer legal protection for their realization, the world is full of denials of claims founded upon people's fundamental freedoms and basic entitlements. Actually, while the whole idea of rights is based upon the expectation that evident violations would lead to contentious action resulting in redress, human rights often remain without effective remedies. This is due to two crucial deficiencies: firstly, the often prevailing inadequacy of law as a check on power, and secondly, the lack of reception of these rights in many cultural and politico-economic contexts.

In terms of the role and rule of law, society is expected to function in such a way that rights are respected, and claims based on entitlements connected to those rights get honoured. Dispute settlement is confined to cases in which there are conflicting claims protected by different rights. In the case of human rights, however, adequate embodiment in positive law is all too often lacking, while they get violated in and from centres of power, too.

There are notable differences in context here. While in the Netherlands, for example, freedom of speech is protected by a historically acquired right, in China it is based on an internationally declared right that is structurally violated from the national political centre. In the case of economic, social and cultural rights general recognition at the centres of power in the global economy is even lacking. The character of human rights as 'declaratory' rather than 'conclusive' concerns economic, social and cultural rights in particular and manifests itself especially in countries in the South. This is not just a matter of socioeconomic context: no jobs, no access to land and hence extreme pressure on scarce productive resources that breeds frustration and aggression rather than recognition of other people's freedoms and needs.

There is also a political setting that finds its background in the history of colonialism and its effects on the distribution and control of power, both internationally and in local contexts. As a result the fight for social justice in a modern economy and polity has a long way to go. Internationally that struggle has not yielded impressive fruits up till now. Over the past two centuries the gaps between the richest and the poorest countries have widened while in absolute terms in the poorest region, sub-Saharan Africa, the number of people living on less than one US dollar a day increased considerably during the nineteen nineties. As a result of decisions taken in the name of economic progress, the world's poor often face increasing hardships from day to day. In that dim light the toughness of the struggle for social justice within so many developing countries could hardly be seen as surprising. Obviously, the human rights venture as envisaged requires laborious law based on functioning legal systems, internationally as well as in domestic settings.

The essence of law is that it binds power to certain norms, implying at the least normative processes of settling disputes. Legal norms then are meant not only to regulate in the sense of securing order but also to reflect what is generally seen as right and hence ought to be enforced. Law, in other words, binds power to a morality that is seen as essential to the integrity of the community as such. This rather idealistic view depicts law as it is meant to be: justice incognito. At the other extreme we find anti-law: the use of legal instruments to institutionalize injustice. Karl Marx saw law as rooted in class relations: 'right can never be higher than the economic structure of society and its cultural development conditioned thereby'. Socioeconomic power, in that view, completely dominates law.

Reality tends to lie somewhere between, on the one hand, the binding of power to norms rooted in morality and, on the other hand, the reflection of existing power relations in the setting and execution of such standards. These dialectics of law and power are appealingly echoed in the way in which the notorious villain Bul Super - a comic figure in Marten Toonder's Adventures of Tom Poes - expresses his view on law: 'right is something crooked that has been twisted'. The issue then, is law's moral foundations and connections.

According to Jurgen Habermas, the impersonal relationships that typify an exchange economy as well as a modern polity, imply that both tend to function as systems, separated from the lifeworld of culture, social interaction and personality. A topical illustration of what this refers to is the organization of agriculture in the European Union and its alienation from the lifeworld of animals and people. Law, then, secures the independence of economy and state from lifeworld structures. It regulates exchange relations through property and contract and institutionalizes the political system by defining bureaucratic positions based on administrative law. Modern law is not grounded in normative rightness but is: positive in the sense of the outcome of established processes of law-making; legalistic, implying an orientation towards rules; and formal, meaning that cases are judged under what has been regulated with a view to 'equal' treatment of 'equal' cases.

Modern law is functional coercion and as such in need of normative justification. This confronts us with the crucial notion of legitimacy. While Weber saw law's claim to legitimacy as based purely on political domination, for Habermas enacted law cannot secure the basis of its legitimacy simply through legality. Indeed, with its many manifestations of illegitimate rule the twentieth century has generally confronted humankind with the complexity of legitimacy as a concept transcending formal-procedural legality.

Grounded in people's conviction that the way power is exercised over them and the way in which they are being ruled are right, legitimacy transforms power into authority. In this light legitimacy becomes not so much a fact but a process. The right procedures (due process) are only one aspect of this; other elements concern the right principles and institutions and an outcome acceptable to those affected by the exercise of power.

In terms of legitimacy the continuous challenge is, in other words, to find law in its 'lifeworld' connection to justice. Notably, that need to transcend purely formal legality is nothing new. Through the ages substantial legitimization has been enhanced by applying the old principles of law-finding: the regulae iuris. They throw light upon concrete cases in which legal rules first have to be determined as applicable and then applied in line with a correct interpretation.

As maxims (maximae propositiones) the rules of law rest on everyday common sense; as concise declarations of the demands of justice (generalia iuris principia) they are rooted in morality. An example of legal common sense is the rule that everything that has come into being through certain causes, can be dissolved by the same causes.

General principles of justice may be illustrated by the rule that without guilt there can be no punishment. Often the regulae combine elements of both logic and fairness, exemplified, for example by the rule that whosoever carries the burden should also be entitled to the benefits. Usually their form is short and succinct while their authority rests on past experience in law-finding. In the difficult task of weighing the different interests involved, the regulae assist those charged with law-making as well as those responsible for law-finding in concrete cases. These rules of law then, exert an immediate appeal to both heart and mind. Thus, Baldus stated that a party in a court case that can invoke a regula iuris might be considered as being prima facie in its right.

While apparently that could be said in the fourteenth century, the regulae have maintained their validity through the ages. For example, the stipulation that no one can change his policy to another person's unfair detriment , acquired a modern translation in the principle of good government which demands that justified expectations as have been raised, cannot be neglected. Paul Scholten has typified such general principles of law as the desk light that may shine so clearly upon a case that what the ceiling light of the statute books could not reveal, suddenly becomes clearly visible.

Some regulae are quite precise, particularly those that pertain to due process. As examples may serve the well-known rule that not just one party but both parties should be heard (audi et alteram partem), and the rule that no one can be a judge in his own case (nemo iudex in sua propria causa). Other regulae are of a highly general character, e.g. the exclamation that freedom is of inestimable value (libertas inaestimabilis res est). A little more concrete, but still common to many topics is the requirement of good faith (bona fides). Beside such rules there are also those which are particular to one topic, e.g. sale can break no rent. As 'the general principles of law recognized by civilized nations' the regulae iuris have been acknowledged as a source of law-finding for the International Court of Justice. But apart from their role as guidelines in adjudication they also play their part in law-making and administration.

While most rules originate in Roman law, many have been incorporated in the Corpus Iuris Canonicis and in subsequent law books as well. Yet, legal incorporation in recognized texts such as Dinus' treatise on the Rules of the Sext is not the essence. Important is not the formal source of a rule of law but its immediate appeal to the legal mind and the moral heart. Principally their role lies in the need for legitimacy rather than pure legality. It is that evident connection to formal and substantial justice through which they may play such a significant part in political, administrative and judicial decision-making.

In a Habermasean framework the regulae may be seen as a first mode of resistance by the lifeworld to a rules-driven jurisprudence. In regard to the various waves of juridification in modern history Habermas himself mentions three distinct ways in which the lifeworld has resisted a strict separation of law from morality. A first response to law as pure formality is embodied in the modern notion of the human being as an individual with rights. This implies legal protection of individual interests against detrimental use of power by others, including the sovereign.

Different subjective rights may well clash, necessitating in concrete cases a weighing of the various interests involved in the light of the normativity embodied in legal rules. Secondly, democratization of the political order tends to confront persons holding office with reactions by those in whose private and public interests power is supposed to be executed. Finally, in modern industrialized countries the social welfare state guarantees freedoms and rights against the economic system. These three modes of resistance to law as pure domination may well be conceived as bridges between systems of functional formality and the lifeworld of (inter)personal normativity. In this address the emphasis is particularly on the first bridge, taken in its normative setting of human rights.

From a legal-philosophical perspective human rights may be seen as connecting general principles of justice with the conception of human beings as individuals with subjective rights. Each distinct human right has a core that relates to human dignity. Behind that core is a general principle connected with public justice in the sense of a communal conviction of what is right and so crucial for the integrity of the public -political community that it ought to be enforced. Examples of such principles of justice as reflected in the International Bill of Rights are liberty, equality, due process (with sub-principles such as habeas corpus and objectivity and impartiality in judicial decision-making), humanity (respect for human life), the integrity of the body, privacy, stability of possessions, participation, etc.

The next step in terms of standard-setting is to elaborate these principles in legal texts aimed at incorporation in different types of domestic law. The relative success of such attempts to further positivize human rights depends firstly on the question whether in the country in question legal systems do function, secondly on their judicial and political openness to the crucial issue of legitimacy as a notion transcending pure formal legality, and thirdly on cultural factors. Indeed, spiritual roots of a culture of human rights have to be found in different social and cultural contexts.

Hence, in accepting their responsibility for the implementation of human rights states are well advised to look for religious and other types of moral support for efforts made within the environment of their specific jurisdiction as well as in an international setting. This applies to the North as well as the South. Particularly problematic in the American setting, for example, is the principle of recognition of need - social justice - that lies behind articles 22 to 25 of the Universal Declaration of Human Rights and the International Covenant on Economic, Social and Cultural Rights.

The struggle for social justice appeals to people's sense of solidarity and collective responsibility. But in the context of a settlers' society like the USA - a country that has such a dominant influence on global culture - it is individual autonomy rather than social justice that dominates legal and political thinking.As we all know, this type of politico-legal thinking is not confined to just the USA. Notably, the culture underlying economic globalization is generally based on possessive individualism rather than social justice.

While the international community still lacks the means to enforce the fundamental freedoms that have been declared as universal rights, basic entitlements for each and every human being apparently cannot acquire a human rights profile by simple declaration. Yet, the formulation of basic entitlements to education, health care, food, clothing, housing and employment as rights has raised expectations and 'rights-based approaches' further increase these. Thus, the world of human rights is a world of unfulfilled expectations.

While, inevitably, human rights have to be incorporated in the systems of our time, a serious concern today is that they have become a typical system of their own: intergovernmental and nongovernmental centres, compliance and complaints procedures with commissions, committees and courts of law, training programmes and academic teaching courses, often quite far removed from lifeworld perspectives. The term 'secular religion' is used in this connection, and that is meant particularly in an institutional sense.

Because in the global struggle to bind all use of power to essential standards we have nothing that could better suit the requirements of protecting people's human dignity in a modern setting. Rhetoric, true, but a strong and morally compelling rhetoric. Rights do, indeed, fulfil the important function of providing legal protection to subjective claims based on recognized interests, and hence incorporation of human rights in functioning legal systems must be seen as essential, but even where this is not yet the case they can still be seen as statements of what is right, an objective moral code, in other words.

At this point an aside is in place: the word 'moral' here concerns the grounding of these rights in morality and does not imply that human rights should be considered as 'moral rights' as opposed to 'legal rights'. It is particularly in political science circles in North America that we find that juxtaposition. The term 'moral rights' stands for rights that cannot be enforced or, in other words, rights without remedies.

Rights are 'performative' and one of the things that make human rights distinct is that, perhaps more than other rights they are particularly performative. The point made earlier is that in many respects the struggle for their implementation is still in its early stages, and hence these rights often cannot offer immediately effective remedies. The word 'right', then, holds a legal significance, signifying that what is confirmed in such terminology is right and ought to be protected by law so as to guarantee enforcement. Like law itself, rights find their meaning in order and justice. As human rights are rooted in justice, their realization is not just a matter of enforcing positive law but a moral issue.

Let us now return to the strategic model on which the global human rights venture is based. International standard-setting and monitoring coupled, principally, with local struggles for enforcement and implementation. In this endeavour international agencies for development cooperation such as the United Nations Development Program (UNDP) have chosen to concentrate their efforts on 'enabling environments' in the sense of enhancing the right type of conditions under which people can exercise their human rights.

It is abundantly clear, however, that many people live in environments which, far from being conducive to local implementation, must be regarded as hostile to any efforts for the protection of basic human dignity. In such disabling conditions human rights tend to function not so much as legal resources but as political instruments to mobilize dissent, protest, opposition and collective action aimed at social and economic reform.

It is particularly in adverse conditions as those pertaining in situations of extreme pressure on scarce resources that a political economy analysis may be enlightening. It implies a meta-juridical approach that looks beyond disciplinary boundaries. Empirically, the triangle economy-polity-law is of central importance. Crucial is the analysis of economic, political and legal aspects of problems and policies at their interface and in their interaction.

Political economy of human rights, then, is a way of looking behind systemic violations and structural non-implementation. Remarkably, its contribution is not restricted to economic, social and cultural rights. Lack of implementation of civil, political and cultural rights, too, has to be assessed in a politico-economic context.

Lederach has pointed, for example, to the 'justice gap' in efforts directed at peace-making. Behind collective violence there often lies a 'root conflict' related to economic aspects of public justice. Apparently, when the violence ends, people expect not only pacification but also serious efforts towards economic justice.Yet, the primary contribution of political economy of human rights lies in the field of socioeconomic rights.

A basic distinction has to be made between rights, entitlements and claims. A right implies neither more nor less than an abstract acknowledgement of claims. Entitlement is concrete: lawful command over a good or service in a specified use. A claim is an actual act of acquirement. For example, owner of a house is generally presumed free to use it. This includes the presumption of an entitlement to live there. Hence he may well claim actual occupancy of those premises. But it is quite possible that another person is already entitled to occupy that house, a tenant, for example. If both claim occupancy at the same time the judge in question will look behind the conflicting claims and weigh the relative strengths of the respective rights as well as the different interests of the parties. If in the light of the rules and the facts the case seems to be unclear, general principles may well provide the clarity that is needed to find the law in this specific dispute.

In the same way in which the relation between abstract rights and concrete entitlements is not mechanical, neither is there an automatic link between entitlements and honoured claims. Usually, in order to claim what one wants certain activities are required within processes of production, distribution and consumption of goods and services: land has to be worked, commodities have to be manufactured and sold, services have to be delivered, consumer goods have to be bought in shops, a door has to be opened with a key, etc. Entitlements provide neither more nor less than access to such processes; actual acquirement also requires activities and action. Suppose a person is homeless simply because she lacks any concrete entitlement to occupy any premises. What then, in terms of concrete entitlements, is the implication of her housing right as defined in article 25 of the UDHR and article 11 of the ICESCR? Unfortunately, this human right does not generally function as a direct source of concrete entitlements. If, however, a homeless individual takes concrete action in order to find a roof above her head, that housing right as recognized in international law, may well play its part. In the Netherlands this is what actually happened in the nineteen-sixties and seventies when squatters began occupying houses that stood empty as the owners used their property for speculative purposes only.

Another type of consequence that might follow from the general housing right is a judicial prohibition to deprive human beings from access to their sole resort without offering an alternative. In Indian public interest litigation, for instance, the Supreme Court has ruled that homeless beggars cannot be simply removed from pavements of streets on which they lay their heads. In short, while generally economic rights have been declared as rights without entitlements, entitlements following from the human right in question can be asserted through concrete action. Human rights, in other words, are transformational, too: they establish a normative framework for processes of social change. As there can be rights without entitlements, the opposite may equally obtain. Thus, a peasant may have lawful access to a plot simply because a relevant authority - e.g. the chief of his tribe - granted this for as long as he works that piece of land. Indeed, institutional relations may also serve as entitlement (sub)systems. Highly relevant in this connection is the relationship between citizens and their state. Generally, state power may serve as a source of many concrete entitlements. However, the state may also interfere negatively in people's entitlements, through expropriation for example. Hence, for the purpose of human rights implementation government policies and actions have to be closely monitored in their effects upon the entitlement positions of those living in daily hardship.

It is the universality of human rights as internationally accepted standards of legitimacy that makes it possible to mobilize international support in struggles against their violation, too. International pressure, through reporting or other types of procedures by the United Nations Special Rapporteur for Housing for example, may well contribute to processes of acquiring actual recognition of people's housing needs.

The possibility of taking human rights abuse to court tends to be underestimated, particularly in regard to economic, social and cultural rights. Although, as has been pointed out, a homeless individual cannot usually sue the state for provision of a house, forced evictions or cutting off essential services can be contested in courts of law. There is a difference, in other words, between a state of non-implementation and a concrete act of violation. Now, if human rights were no more than subjective rights albeit of a special type, the four major areas of impunity characterizing the human rights deficit mentioned at the beginning of this presentation would have a paralysing effect on the whole venture. In that case the issue would be confined to justiciability.

Human rights, must be seen not merely as subjective rights - to be enforced through claims based on entitlements derived from them - but also as general principles of justice. In the latter meaning they may play their part in adjudication too, not as a direct basis for the acceptance of certain claims but to throw light upon a case, in the same way in which the old regulae iuris perform that function. Let us take, for example, the damages suffered by small fishermen when, in the name of development, big trawlers are introduced that go into the shallow waters, destroying the breeding grounds for the fish that forms the basis of their livelihoods.

It is true that in contentious action these people may fail to get recognition of claims based on a subjective 'right to development' but in concrete litigation procedures the right to development may well be invoked in order to determine responsibility for a tort. Thus far, the emphasis has been on law in a modern universalistic sense, i.e. enforcement of rules through regularized mechanisms. If, however, the realization of fundamental norms binding the use of power were purely dependent on formal legal processes, in many places deficits in the enforcement of crucial standards would be much worse. Fortunately, however, law can also work through informal mechanisms or, in another terminology, as living law. While 'law' manifests itself as regulation of power, living law has the nature of 'anti-power'.

An illustration may be taken from the social history of slavery in Barbados. Records of slave births and sales show that from the end of the eighteenth century onwards infants were no longer sold apart from their mothers and the nuclear family became a common phenomenon among slaves, implying among other things that husbands and wives were also not sold separately. Apparently female slaves regarded motherhood as 'a customary right'; yet there was no justiciability whatsoever since slaves were regarded as chattel and certainly not recognized as legal subjects. What we come across here is noticeable self-enforcement of human rights by informal means.

Moreover, human rights function not only as legal resources but as political instruments: standards of legitimacy, applicable to any use of power, whether by the state or by non-state actors. The processes through which this is effectuated may have a formal as well as an informal character. Besides living law, in other words, we also touch upon living politics as a way of confronting power with human rights standards. To illustrate the meaning of living politics it may be helpful to juxtapose two distinct situations: a parliament without a free press means dead politics, a free press without a parliament would lead to living politics. In the case of the fishermen described above, those in power might feel aware of a potential resistance that is still submerged but would be likely to get activated when the local population see their fishing grounds destroyed. Such a hidden potential, based as it is on strong feelings of justice and injustice, might discourage big trawlers from fishing in shallow waters. It is, indeed, in regard to non-state actors, too, that living politics is likely to become increasingly relevant.

Globalization today also affects interpretations of legitimacy. As a consequence, principles in regard to the use of power become more and more general in the sense of being shared in the whole ius gentium. In regard to human rights this opens the way to more inductive approaches. To clarify: a deductive approach derives concrete rights from international treaties and other formal sources; an inductive approach starts from what people see themselves as the fundamental freedoms and entitlements that everyone should enjoy. Such a growing focus on lifeworld contexts also applies to processes of legitimization.

Institutional decisions that affect the lives of people are more and more confronted with universal standards of legitimacy, including the old regulae iuris and modern human rights. While the international venture for the protection of human rights has been set up with particular emphasis on the role of the state, today there is a growing attention to human rights observance by non-state actors. Since historically the applicability of rules of justice has never been confined to the state, such a development should not surprise us. Moreover, in the major challenge of bridging functional systems and lifeworld morality, states and non-state actors need each other.

3

Universal Declaration of Human Rights

Adopted by General Assembly Resolution

217 A (III) of 10 December 1948

Whereas it is essential, if man is not to be compelled to have recourse, as a last resort, to rebellion against tyranny and oppression, that human rights should be protected by the rule of law.

The importance of ensuring that human rights are protected under the rule of law has been emphasised by the United Nations since the drafting of the Universal Declaration of Human Rights, and has guided the Organisation in its activities for the promotion and protection of human rights ever since. This is most evident in the work of the United Nations Programme of Advisory Services and Technical Cooperation in the Field of Human Rights. This programme, as described below, has been engaged since 1955 in assisting States, at their request, in the building and strengthening of national structures which have a direct impact on the overall observance of human rights and the maintenance of the rule of law.

A decade after the entry into force of the Charter of the United Nations, and after some early ad hoc human rights assistance activities, the General Assembly officially established the United Nations Programme of Advisory Services in the Field of Human Rights (resolution 926 (X) of 14 December 1955). Thereby, the General Assembly specifically authorised the Secretary-General to make provision, at the request of governments, for assistance in the field of human rights, including advisory services of experts, fellowships and scholarships, and seminars. Subsequently, the General Assembly increased the services available under the programme to include regional and national human rights training courses. On the basis of these resolutions, activities under the programme have been carried out in numerous countries in each of the world's regions for some 40 years.

The programme was further strengthened when the Voluntary Fund for Advisory Services and Technical Assistance in the Field of Human Rights (subsequently renamed Voluntary Fund for Technical Cooperation in the Field of Human Rights) was established by the Secretary-General in November 1987 pursuant to the Commission on Human Rights resolution 1987/38 of 10 March 1987 and the Economic and Social Council decision 1987/147 of 29 May 1987. The objective of the trust fund is to provide additional financial support for practical activities focused on the implementation of international conventions and other international instruments on human rights promulgated by the United Nations, its specialised agencies or regional organisations.

In accordance with relevant Commission on Human Rights resolutions, practical activities to be financed by the Voluntary Fund include:

a) support for international cooperation aimed at establishing and strengthening national and regional institutions and infrastructures which will have a long-term impact on improved implementation of international conventions and other international instruments on human rights promulgated by the United Nations, its specialised agencies or regional organisations;

b) expert and technical assistance to governments with a view to creating and developing the necessary infrastructures to meet international human rights standards;

c) projects and programmes that can play a catalytic role in the practical realisation of internationally recognised human rights standards;

d) projects for legal protection and strengthening of the independence of the judiciary;

e) comprehensive needs assessments and overall country programmes, including specific projects aimed at strengthening the human rights infrastructure of a country.

The technical assistance programme financed under the Voluntary Fund is therefore a comprehensive programme providing practical assistance for the building of national and regional human rights infrastructures. Programme components focus on the incorporation of international human rights standards into national laws and policies, and on the establishment or strengthening of national institutions capable of promoting and protecting human rights and democracy under the rule of law. Such assistance now takes the form of expert advisory services, training courses, workshops and seminars, fellowships, grants, the provision of information and documentation and the assessment of domestic human rights needs.

For its part, the World Conference on Human Rights, throughout the Vienna Declaration and Programme of Action which it adopted in June 1993, recognised the importance of advisory services and technical assistance for human rights and called for enhancement of the programme.

With regard to technical cooperation, for example, the Declaration and Programme of Action call for the implementation of plans of action at the national level for the promotion and protection of human rights through the establishment of a comprehensive United Nations programme (part II, paras. 68-69). The Technical Cooperation Programme, according to the Declaration, should be strengthened. The Declaration further states that the Centre for Human Rights should make available to States, upon request, technical and financial assistance, in particular for the elaboration and implementation of coherent and comprehensive plans of action. These plans of action would integrate activities aimed at: (a) strengthening the institutions of human rights and democracy; (b) reforming penal and correctional establishments; (c) the legal protection of human rights; (d) education and training of officials, lawyers, judges, security forces and others in human rights; (e) broad-based education and public information for promoting respect for human rights; and (f) other means of promoting the good functioning of the rule of law.

Funding and Administration of the Technical Cooperation Programme

The Programme of Technical Cooperation in the Field of Human Rights is funded from the regular budget of the United Nations and from the United Nations Voluntary

Fund for Technical Cooperation in the Field of Human Rights, which began operating in 1988 and to date has received more than US$ 19 million in pledges and contributions. In addition to financing from the regular budget and the Voluntary Fund, specific projects are sometimes funded by partners of the Centre for Human Rights in the United Nations system.

Whatever the source of funding, projects are implemented within the common context of a single, unified and comprehensive programme, administered by the Centre for Human Rights. While, consistent with resolutions of the Commission on Human Rights, a distinction is maintained between projects financed under the regular budget and those financed by the Voluntary Fund for purposes of accountability, reporting and budgetary information, the common substance and policy of the programme remain.

Programme development, implementation, support and follow-up are carried out by the Technical Cooperation Branch of the Centre for Human Rights, under the direction of the Assistant Secretary-General for Human Rights. The United Nations High Commissioner for Human Rights holds overall responsibility for the programme, under the authority of the Secretary-General. The High Commissioner is mandated, under General Assembly resolution 48/141 of 20 December 1993, to provide, through the Centre for Human Rights, advisory services and technical assistance at the request of States and, where appropriate, regional human rights organisations, with a view to supporting actions and programmes in the field of human rights. He is also responsible, *inter alia*, for coordinating human rights promotion and protection activities throughout the United Nations system.

In a further important development, the Commission on Human Rights, in its resolution 1993/87 of 10 March 1993 (para. 18), requested the Secretary-General to appoint a board of trustees to assume the administration of the Voluntary Fund. The board of trustees was established in December 1993.

The Programme Approach

Technical cooperation activities are seen by the United Nations as a complement to, but never a substitute for, the monitoring and investigating activities of the human rights programme. As emphasised in various reports of the Secretary-General on the subject, and in Commission on Human Rights resolution 1995/53 of 3 March 1995 (preamble), the provision of advisory services and technical assistance does not reduce a government's responsibility to account for the human rights situation and, whenever applicable, would not exempt it from monitoring through the various procedures established by the United Nations. Indeed, action by special rapporteurs of the Commission on Human Rights often takes place in parallel with projects of advisory services and technical assistance.

While the Technical Cooperation Programme occasionally provides grants in support of projects initiated by non-governmental organisations, governments and regional human rights organisations, it is not, in the first instance, a funding source for projects developed outside the Centre for Human Rights. Rather, it is a source of substantive advice and assistance in the field of human rights, within the framework of a comprehensive programme which cooperates with governments, at their request, through Centre-generated needs assessments and projects designed in cooperation with recipient countries.

The Centre for Human Rights, in most cases, responds to a government's request by conducting a careful assessment of the country's particular human rights assistance needs. Assistance programmes are then designed to address those needs in a comprehensive and coordinated way. The Centre directly implements all projects for which it has unique or specific competence, drawing on the considerable expertise developed by its staff in the relevant areas, and serves as a focal point and coordinator for other programme elements relating to the human rights needs of the country concerned. This comprehensive approach was first described in the 1993 report of the Secretary-General on advisory services in the field of human rights, and was further elaborated in his 1994 report.

Content of the Programme

Guided by successive General Assembly and Commission on Human Rights resolutions, and by the nature of State requests themselves, the Technical Cooperation Programme gradually developed capacities for assistance in a range of areas, which now provide a useful framework for national efforts directed at strengthening human rights and the rule of law. Thus the Centre for Human Rights now adopts a comprehensive approach to human rights institution building, which sees as fundamental the following constituent elements for national efforts to secure the protection of human rights under the rule of law:

a) a strong Constitution, which, as the highest law of the land, *inter alia*:

i) incorporates internationally recognised human rights and fundamental freedoms, as enumerated in the International Bill of Human Rights;

ii) establishes effective and justifiable remedies at law for violations of those rights;

iii) empowers an independent judiciary, consistent with the Basic Principles on the Independence of the Judiciary;

iv) provides for nondiscrimination on the basis of race, colour, gender, language, religion, political or other opinion, national or social origin, property, birth or other status and which protects national minorities;

v) establishes national human rights institutions, such as an office of the ombudsman or an independent human rights commission, consistent with the United Nations Principles relating to the status of national institutions;

vi) provides for the applicability of international human rights treaty obligations in domestic law;

vii) defines and limits the powers of government and its various branches, *vis-a-vis* each other and the people.

b) a strong electoral system, which, *inter alia*:

i) assures that the will of the people is the basis of the authority of government;

ii) assures the right of everyone to take part in the government of his or her country, either directly or through freely chosen representatives;

iii) assures equal access to public service, including elective public service;

iv) provides for periodic and genuine elections;

v) guarantees universal and equal suffrage;

vi) guarantees the secrecy of the ballot;

vii) secures an electoral atmosphere which is free of intimidation and respectful of certain prerequisite rights, such as freedom of opinion, expression, information, assembly and association;

viii) provides for nondiscrimination in the area of political rights;

ix) provides for independent review of alleged irregularities;

x) provides for objective, unbiased and independent electoral administration;

xi) provides for the transfer of power to victorious parties and candidates under the law.

c) a strong legal framework, under the Constitution, which protects human rights and democracy and provides for effective redress in all key areas, including, *inter alia*:

i) fair immigration, nationality and asylum laws which are consistent with relevant international standards;

ii) penal laws and laws of criminal procedure which respect and uphold international standards for human rights in the administration of justice;

iii) electoral laws which take account of the above concerns;

iv) prison laws and regulations which are consistent with the Standard Minimum Rules for the Treatment of Prisoners and other relevant international instruments;

v) laws for the protection of minorities, women, children, indigenous people and other vulnerable groups, which take into account their special status and international standards for their protection, and which outlaw and address the effects of discrimination,

vi) laws protecting free association and assembly;

vii) security legislation which is consistent with international standards, and which protects non-derogable human rights;

viii) laws on the judiciary, on legal practice and on prosecution which reflect the standards embodied in the Basic Principles on the Independence of the Judiciary, the Basic Principles on the Role of Lawyers, the Guidelines on the Role of Prosecutors and other United Nations standards on the administration of justice;

ix) laws, guidelines and directives which govern the conduct of police and other security forces, consistent with the Code of Conduct for Law Enforcement Officials, the Basic Principles on the Use of Force and Firearms by Law Enforcement Officials and other relevant international standards;

x) fair procedures for the settlement of civil disputes under the law, and fair administrative laws, procedures and institutions, consistent with international human rights standards;

xi) any other laws which may have a direct impact on the realisation of internationally guaranteed human rights.

d) strong national human rights institutions, including independent commissions on human rights and ombudsman offices, with structures and functions consistent with the United Nations Principles relating to the status of national institutions, as well as strong national human rights research and training institutes;

e) a strong judiciary, which is independent, adequately empowered, adequately financed, adequately equipped, and adequately trained to uphold human rights in the administration of justice;

f) a military which has ultimate allegiance to the Constitution and laws of the land, and to the democratic government, and which is trained in and committed to the principles of human rights and humanitarian lawattending legitimate military duties;

g) effective and accessible mechanisms for the resolution of conflicts between and among citizens and groups in society and State organs;

h) full incorporation into the international human rights system, including through ratification of or accession to international human rights treaties and training of government officials in implementing and reporting under those treaties;

i) a society which is educated in its rights and responsibilities, including through national human rights curricula in primary, secondary and post-secondary education, and teachers trained in education for human rights and democracy;

j) a strong civil society, including adequately trained, equipped, financed and organised non-governmental human rights organisations, women's groups, labour unions and community organisations.

Taken together, these essential elements provide for a legal and institutional framework which will best serve to entrench the rule of law in society and thereby secure the effective enjoyment of human rights and democracy. In recognition of this, the Technical Cooperation Programme of the Centre for Human Rights, in partnership with other United Nations organs, governments and non-governmental organisations, offers support to States seeking to strengthen these elements. As already indicated, such support takes the form of comprehensive country programmes and targeted projects, in the form of advisory services of experts, training courses, workshops and seminars, information and documentation projects, fellowships and some forms of financial assistance, in the substantive areas described below:

1. *National Plans of Action*

In the Vienna Declaration and Programme of Action which it adopted in June 1993, the World Conference on Human Rights recommended that the Centre for Human Rights, through its advisory services and technical assistance activities, assist States in the preparation of plans of action at the national level. In accordance with that recommendation, the Technical Cooperation Programme can make available expert assistance in the elaboration of such plans, and in their implementation.

2. *Constitutional Assistance*

Under this programme component, the Centre for Human Rights provides assistance for the inclusion of human rights norms in national constitutions, and can play a facilitative role in encouraging national consensus on the elements to be incorporated in those constitutions. Assistance for these purposes may take the form of advisory services of experts, the organisation of conferences, provision of human rights information and documentation, or support for public information campaigns to ensure the involvement of all sectors of society.

Issues addressed in the Centre's constitutional activities include legislative drafting and constitutional law; the drafting of bills of rights; the provision of justifiable remedies under the law; options for the allocation and separation of governmental powers; the independence of the judiciary; and the role of the judiciary in overseeing the police and prison systems.

3. *Electoral Assistance*

The Centre for Human Rights has been involved in electoral assistance, through its Technical Cooperation Programme, for more than five years. Since 1990, the Centre has provided electoral assistance to Romania (1990-1992), Albania (1991), Lesotho (1991-1993), Eritrea (1992), Angola (1992), Cambodia (1992), Malawi (1992-1993) and South Africa (1993). In addition, the Centre has prepared guidelines for analysis of electoral laws and procedures, published a handbook on human rights and elections, developed draft guidelines for human rights assessments of requests for electoral assistance, and carried out a number of public information activities relating to human rights and elections.

4. *Legislative Reform Assistance*

As a further component of the Technical Cooperation Programme, the Centre for Human Rights makes available international experts and specialised staff to assist governments in the reform of legislation which has a clear impact on human rights and fundamental freedoms. The goal of such assistance is to bring such laws into conformity with international standards, as identified in United Nations and regional human rights instruments. The Centre provides comments on drafts provided by the requesting government, as well as drafting recommendations, which may include comparative reference to similar laws in other jurisdictions.

Appropriate subjects under this programme component include penal codes, codes of criminal procedure, prison regulations, laws regarding minority protection, laws affecting freedom of expression, association and assembly, immigration and nationality laws, laws on the judiciary and legal practice, security legislation, and, in general, any law which might have an impact, directly or indirectly, on the realisation of internationally protected human rights.

5. *Assistance in the Establishment and Strengthening of National Institutions*

As its role has been defined by the Commission on Human Rights, a central objective of the Technical Cooperation Programme is to consolidate and strengthen the role which national institutions can play in the promotion and protection of human rights. Assistance to national institutions under the programme takes several forms. The Centre for Human Rights offers its services to governments which are considering or in the process of establishing a national human rights institution.

Other activities relating to national institutions under the programme are not oriented towards a particular country or institution but are, instead, aimed at promoting the concept of national human rights institutions and encouraging their development. To this end, the Centre has produced information materials and a practical manual for those involved in the establishment and administration of national institutions. The Centre has also conducted a number of seminars and workshops to provide government officials with both information and expertise in the structure and functioning of such bodies. These events have also served as useful forums in which to promote the exchange of information and experience concerning the establishment and operation of national institutions.

The Centre for Human Rights has developed a comprehensive programme of action for technical assistance to national institutions which now guides the elaboration and implementation of all assistance projects to national institutions. In developing this programme, the Centre was guided by the Principles relating to the status of national institutions endorsed by the Commission on Human Rights in its resolution 1992/54 of 3 March 1992 and subsequently by the General Assembly in its resolution 48/134 of 20 December 1993. The programme of action sets out four specific objectives: to promote the concept of national human rights institutions; to assist in the creation of effective institutions; to assist in the strengthening of existing institutions; and to foster cooperation between institutions.

Assistance provided by the Centre for strengthening national institutions may include training of staff; advice on the domestic implementation of international human rights instruments; training and assistance in the drafting of reports to United Nations treaty bodies; training and information on the effective investigation of human rights violations; training in conflict resolution; assistance in the establishment of cooperative relationships with appropriate partners; information on obtaining and managing resources; assistance in conducting reviews and evaluations; and the provision of human rights fellowships for members and staff of national institutions.

6. *Administration of Justice: Judges, Magistrates, Lawyers, Prosecutors, Police and Prison Officials*

The Centre for Human Rights, through its Technical Cooperation Programme, has been involved for many years in the training of judges, lawyers, prosecutors, police officers and prison personnel in the area of human rights in the administration of justice.

The purposes of these courses are to familiarise participants with international standards for human rights in the administration of justice; to facilitate examination of humane and effective techniques for the performance of law enforcement, penal and judicial functions in a democratic society; and to prepare participants to include this information in their own training activities.

This approach to professional training for human rights in the administration of justice has, for three years, been undergoing in-field testing by the Centre in its technical cooperation activities in a number of countries, and has been subjected to a series of revisions on the basis of that experience.

a) Law Enforcement Officials

The Centre's courses for law enforcement officials cover a variety of topics, including the following: international sources, systems and standards for human rights in the administration of criminal justice; the duties and guiding principles of ethical police conduct in democracies; the use of force and firearms in law enforcement; the crime of torture; effective methods of legal and ethical interviewing; human rights during arrest and pre-trial detention; and the legal status and rights of the accused.

b) Prison Officials

Course topics in this category include: minimum standards for facilities for prisoners and detainees; prison health issues, including AIDS and the HIV virus; and special categories of prisoners and detainees, including juveniles and women.

c) Judges, Magistrates, Lawyers and Prosecutors

Topics offered in courses for this group include: international sources, systems and standards for human rights in the administration of justice; human rights during criminal investigations, arrest and pre-trial detention; the independence of judges and lawyers; the elements of a fair trial; juvenile justice; protection of the rights of women in the administration of justice; and human rights under states of emergency.

7. *Human Rights Training for the Armed Forces*

It is essential for the good functioning of the rule of law that the armed forces be bound by the Constitution and other laws of the land, that they answer to the democratic government and that they are trained in and committed to the principles of human rights and humanitarian law attending their legitimate functions in society. The Centre for Human Rights has carried out a number of training activities for military officers.

Certainly, traditional military training has included, in many cases, some attention to the laws of war, including the four Geneva Conventions of 12 August 1949. Human rights training *per se*, however, has been conspicuously absent. Indeed, not uncommon in some military circles is the notion that human rights training and sensitisation are inconsistent with effective military training. Soldiers, for this way of thinking, are warriors, and the waging of war is, by its very nature, contrary to human rights. The Centre's approach to military training takes issue with this notion for two reasons. First, international human rights standards, including but not always limited to humanitarian law, do apply in situations of armed conflict. Secondly, the duties of modern professional soldiers are not limited to the waging of war. Rather, increasingly, they include civil policing duties, the maintenance of order and public safety under states of emergency, and assignment to international peace-keeping operations. The effective, professional and humane performance of these duties requires a knowledge of and sensitisation to human rights standards, as well as the skills to apply them in the daily work of the military.

8. *Human Rights Support to Parliaments*

National parliaments have, under the Technical Cooperation Programme, received direct training and other support designed to assist them in carrying out their important human rights functions. This programme component addresses a variety of crucial issues, including information on national human rights legislation, parliamentary human rights committees, ratifications of and accessions to international human rights instruments, and, in general, the role of parliament in promoting and protecting human rights.

9. *Curriculum Development and Education for Human Rights*

The Centre for Human Rights is in the process of developing curricula for education on human rights for the primary, secondary and university levels, and for non-formal levels of education. These activities are intended to assist in the building of a human rights culture by encouraging the inclusion of human rights concepts in existing programmes; assisting in the adaptation or modification of curricula where necessary; and providing instruction and assistance to those persons centrally involved in the human rights education process.

There are several means by which these objectives are pursued. The first is teacher training, whereby the Centre offers programmes of training for both primary and secondary school teachers. Courses can also be constructed to accommodate other groups in a position to promote human rights education and sensitise others in this field, such as teacher trainers, directors of schools or teacher-resource centres, and inspectors and teachers within the ministry concerned with curriculum development and education.

10. *Treaty Reporting and International Obligations and Training of Government Officials*

The Centre for Human Rights regularly organises training activities to enable government officials to prepare properly reports required under the various international human rights treaties to which their State is a party. In some cases, courses in reporting obligations are offered at the national or regional level. In others, the Centre provides fellowships for government officials to travel to Geneva, where training courses for several countries are held. During these courses, participants are able to take part in workshops with experts from the various treaty-monitoring committees, as well as with relevant staff of the Centre. In some cases, they are given the opportunity to sit as observers during meetings of the treaty bodies themselves. In every case, participants are provided with a copy of the Centre's *Manual on Human Rights Reporting*.

In accordance with the Centre's standard approach to training, course participants are engaged in practical exercises, which allow them to test the drafting skills imparted during the course. Separate course segments are offered for the International Covenant on Civil and Political Rights; the International Covenant on Economic, Social and Cultural Rights; the Convention on the Rights of the Child; the Convention against Torture and Other Cruel, Inhuman or Degrading Treatment or Punishment; the International Convention on the Elimination of All Forms of Racial Discrimination; the Convention on the Elimination of All Forms of Discrimination against Women; and the International Convention on the Protection of the Rights of All Migrant Workers and Members of Their Families.

11. Support to NGOs and Civil Society

National and international non-governmental human rights organisations (NGOs) are key actors in the Technical Cooperation Programme. NGOs both assist in the delivery of assistance, and benefit as recipients of it.

Thus, in furthering the programme's goal of strengthening civil society, the Centre for Human Rights is increasingly being called upon by governments and others to provide assistance to national NGOs, in the context of its country activities, by soliciting their input, including them as invitees in seminars and training courses, and supporting appropriate projects developed by them.

12. *Information and Documentation Projects*

The Technical Cooperation Programme also provides assistance in the form of provision of human rights information and documentation, and the building of capacity to utilise and manage such materials properly. This includes direct provision of documentation, translated where necessary into local languages; training in human rights informatics; and assistance in computerisation of national and regional human rights offices.

Assistance can also be provided to national libraries in acquiring human rights books and documentation, and support can be given for the establishment and functioning of national or regional human rights documentation centres.

13. *Regional Institutions and Activities*

The Technical Cooperation Programme also focuses on the development of human rights infrastructures at the regional level. This is done primarily through the organisation of regional workshops and seminars, and through support to regional human rights institutions.

The Centre for Human Rights also provides support, through the Voluntary Fund for Technical Cooperation in the Field of Human Rights, for regional human rights institutions involved in educational activities, including direct support to the African Commission on Human and Peoples' Rights, the Arab Institute of Human Rights and the African Centre for Democracy and Human Rights Studies.

14. *Peace-keeping and Training of International Civil Servants*

The Technical Cooperation Programme has recently expanded its activities, in accordance with the Vienna Declaration and Programme of Action adopted by the World Conference on Human Rights in June 1993, to include human rights support within the United Nations system. In the area of peace-keeping, for example, the programme has already provided various forms of assistance to major United Nations missions in Cambodia, Eritrea, Mozambique, Haiti, South Africa, the countries of the former Yugoslavia and Angola. Such assistance has included, variously, the provision of human rights information, legislative analysis, training and advisory services.

Efforts are currently under way to conclude a series of agreements with a number of United Nations specialised agencies, the outcome of which is expected to be an increased level of cooperation between the programme and other United Nations organs engaged in human rights-related activities, for example through the provision of human rights training to staff of those agencies.

15. *Needs Assessments for Human Rights, Democracy and the Rule of Law*

Under the programme approach of the Centre for Human Rights to the provision of technical assistance, discussed above, the Centre responds to most government requests by conducting a careful assessment of the country's particular human rights assistance needs. Assistance programmes are then designed to address those needs in a comprehensive and coordinated way.

Needs-assessment missions conducted by the Centre are typically composed of carefully selected international experts, accompanied by staff of the Technical Cooperation Branch. During such missions, a wide range of parties are consulted in the country, including both governmental and non-governmental organisations and individuals.

The Centre also carries out periodic and post-implementation evaluations of country programmes, in order that their effect may be gauged and follow-up plans developed. These activities are seen by the Centre as crucial to ongoing efforts to strengthen and improve the Technical Cooperation Programme.

16. *Human Rights Fellowships*

General Assembly resolution 926 (X) of 14 December 1955, which officially established the advisory services programme, made direct provision for human rights fellowships. Under the programme, fellowships are awarded only to candidates nominated by their governments, and are financed under the regular budget for advisory services.

The Secretary-General annually sends out invitations to Member States to submit nominations for fellowships. Governments are reminded that nominees should be directly involved in functions affecting human rights, particularly in the administration of justice. The Secretary-General also draws their attention to concerns expressed by the General Assembly, in many of its resolutions, with regard to the rights of women, and encourages the nomination of women candidates. The principle of equitable geographical distribution is taken into account and priority is given to candidates from States which have never benefited from the fellowship programme, or which have not done so in recent years.

Participants receive intensive training in a variety of human rights issues. They are encouraged to exchange experience among themselves, and are requested to evaluate the fellowship programme, to present individual oral reports, and to prepare recommendations for their superiors on the basis of information acquired during the programme. Finally, in accordance with the policy and procedure governing the administration of United Nations fellowships, each participant is required to submit a comprehensive final report to the Centre for Human Rights on subjects directly related to their field of activity.

System-wide Cooperation

The Technical Cooperation Programme enjoys close cooperation with non-governmental organisations, regional institutions, universities, and a number of United Nations specialised agencies and human rights treaty and Charter-based bodies, as well as with the International Committee of the Red Cross. This cooperation has been further enhanced by the new approach of the Centre for Human Rights to needs assessment and project formulation, which involves the full partnership of all organisations and States engaged in human rights assistance. In pursuing an integrated and coordinated approach to human rights, the programme has sought to solidify a cooperative framework which includes the sharing of expertise and resources from all available sources.

Under the United Nations programme approach, the Centre works closely with other United Nations agencies and programmes active in the country concerned, cooperating with the Organisation's Resident Coordinator in ensuring that the Centre's contribution is part of a coordinated United Nations-system intervention and complementary to the projects of other actors in support of the Government's goals, programmes and plans of action. The Centre's technical cooperation activities are therefore placed in the context of a single, unified pursuit of national development objectives through cohesive national programmes which merge United Nations-system inputs with national inputs and those of other actors to achieve government objectives for the promotion and protection of human rights. In every case, the focus is on capacity building, aimed at sustained development progress and the eventual obsolescence of external assistance.

The Technical Cooperation Programme is a vital element within the United Nations system of comprehensive assistance for the strengthening of the rule of law, on the basis of relevant United Nations standards embodied in half a century of human rights standard setting by the Organisation.

The Centre for Human Rights, which develops and implements the programme under the overall direction of the High Commissioner for Human Rights, is the only unit within the United Nations system which is specifically and exclusively charged with institutional responsibility for human rights. This includes gathering and analysing information on the human rights situation in all countries and (through the various official human rights bodies) keeping such situations under periodic review; providing substantive services to United Nations bodies in the development of international human rights standards; assessing the human rights needs, including institutional needs, of individual Member States; developing technical cooperation programmes aimed at building and strengthening national human rights and legal infrastructures; and producing human rights information and training materials.

In addition, in connection with its mandated functions, the Centre for Human Rights continually gathers information and materials on the human rights activities of Member States, inter-governmental and non-governmental organisations, specialised institutions and other United Nations actors.

All these capacities are the bases for the Centre's Technical Cooperation Programme and for its efforts to assist States in strengthening the rule of law in their respective jurisdictions.

4

International Covenant on Economic, Social and Cultural Rights (ICESCR)

The International Covenant on Economic, Social and Cultural Rights was adopted and opened for signature, ratification and accession by General Assembly resolution 2200 A (XXI) of 16 December 1966, following almost 20 years of drafting debates. It finally gained the force of law a decade later, entering into force on 3 January 1976.

The Covenant contains some of the most significant international legal provisions establishing economic, social and cultural rights, including rights relating to work in just and favourable conditions, to social protection, to an adequate standard of living, to the highest attainable standards of physical and mental health, to education and to enjoyment of the benefits of cultural freedom and scientific progress.

As on 12 April 1996, 133 States had ratified the Covenant, thereby voluntarily undertaking to implement its norms and provisions.

Compliance by States parties with their obligations under the Covenant and the level of implementation of the rights and duties in question is monitored by the Committee on Economic, Social and Cultural Rights.

The Committee works on the basis of many sources of information, including reports submitted by States parties and information from United Nations specialised agencies—International Labour Organisation, United Nations Educational, Scientific and Cultural Organisation, World Health Organisation, Food and Agriculture Organisation of the United Nations—from the Office of the United Nations High Commissioner for Refugees, and from the United Nations Centre for Human Settlements (Habitat) and others. It also receives information from non-governmental and community-based organisations working in States which have ratified the Covenant, from international human rights and other non-governmental organisations, from other United Nations treaty bodies, and from generally available literature.

Substantive Provisions of the International Covenant on Economic, Social and Cultural Rights Self-determination

Article 1

1. All peoples have the right of self-determination. By virtue of that right they freely determine their political status and freely pursue their economic, social and cultural development.

2. All peoples may, for their own ends, freely dispose of their natural wealth and resources without prejudice to any obligations arising out of international

economic cooperation, based upon the principle of mutual benefit, and international law. In no case may a people be deprived of its own means of subsistence.

3. The States Parties to the present Covenant, including those having responsibility for the administration of Non-Self-Governing and Trust Territories, shall promote the realisation of the right of self-determination, and shall respect that right, in conformity with the provisions of the Charter of the United Nations.

Article one of the Covenant is worded in precisely the same terminology as article one of its sister text, the International Covenant on Civil and Political Rights. The self-determination provisions in common article one are particularly important because the realisation of this right is a fundamental prerequisite for the effective guarantee and observance of individual human rights and is pivotal in securing and strengthening human rights protection measures.

The right to self-determination is a cornerstone of the international legal system, and has been a premier concern of the international community since the creation of the United Nations in 1945, particularly in regard to issues such as independence, non-interference and democracy. This right has both external and internal dimensions and has been the subject of some controversy in recent years, as it is increasingly asserted by groups within countries, as distinct from ex-colonies and occupied countries.

As far as the rights contained in the Covenant are concerned, the right of peoples freely to pursue their economic, social and cultural development includes freedom to carry on economic, social and cultural activities.

Obligations of States Parties

Article 2

1. Each State Party to the present Covenant undertakes to take steps, individually and through international assistance and cooperation, especially economic and technical, to the maximum of its available resources, with a view to achieving progressively the full realisation of the rights recognised in the present Covenant by all appropriate means, including particularly the adoption of legislative measures.
2. The States parties to the present Covenant undertake to guarantee that the rights enunciated in the present Covenant will be exercised without discrimination of any kind as to race, colour, sex, language, religion, political or other opinion, national or social origin property, birth or other status.
3. Developing countries, with due regard to human rights and their national economy, may determine to what extent they would guarantee the economic rights recognised in the present Covenant to non-nationals.

Article 2 is one of the most important articles of the Covenant because it outlines the nature of States parties' legal obligations under the Covenant and determines how they must approach the implementation of the substantive rights contained in articles 6 to 15.

Any analysis of obligations relating to economic, social and cultural rights cannot be isolated from the obligations inherent in securing the individual entitlements of the beneficiaries of the right(s) in question. Most frequently, obligations are divided into 'layers' reflecting duties to (a) respect, (b) protect, (c) promote, and (d) fulfil each of the rights contained in the Covenant. Each of these legal responsibilities can take on more specific obligations of 'conduct' (e.g., action or inaction) and obligations of 'result' (e.g., ends).

The provision from article 2, paragraph 1, requires all States parties to begin immediately to take measures towards the full enjoyment by everyone of all the rights in the Covenant. The adoption of legislation will, in many cases, be indispensable if economic, social and cultural rights are to be made real, but laws alone are not a sufficient response at the national level. Administrative, judicial, policy, economic, social and educational measures and many other steps will be required by governments in order to ensure these rights to all.

Under article 2, paragraph 1, States parties are legally obliged to undertake legislative action in some instances, particularly when existing laws are clearly incompatible with the obligations assumed under the Covenant. This would be the case when, for instance, a law in a given country was patently discriminatory or had the express effect of preventing the enjoyment of any of the rights in the Covenant, or when legislation allowed the violation of rights, especially in terms of negative duties of States. Laws allowing governments forcibly to remove people from their homes, evicting them without due process of law, would have to be amended in order to bring domestic legislation into conformity with the Covenant.

The 'progressive obligation' component of the Covenant is often mistakenly taken to imply that only once a State reaches a certain level of economic development must the rights established under the Covenant be realised. This is not the intent of this clause.

Rather, the duty in question obliges all States parties, notwithstanding their level of national wealth, to move immediately and as quickly as possible towards the realisation of economic, social and cultural rights. This clause should never be interpreted as allowing States to defer indefinitely efforts to ensure the enjoyment of the rights laid down in the Covenant.

Whereas certain rights, by their nature, may be more apt to be implemented in terms of the 'progressive obligation' rule, many obligations under the Covenant are clearly required to be implemented immediately. This would apply especially to non-discrimination provisions and to the obligation of States parties to refrain from actively violating economic, social and cultural rights or withdrawing legal and other protection relating to those rights.

The Committee on Economic, Social and Cultural Rights has asserted that this duty exists independently of an increase in available resources and thus recognises that all existing resources must be devoted in the most effective way possible to the realisation of the rights enshrined in the Covenant.

Like the 'progressive realisation' provision, this standard is also used to justify the non-enjoyment of rights. However, as recognised in the Limburg Principles on the Implementation of the International Covenant on Economic, Social and Cultural Rights, this requirement obliges States parties to ensure minimum subsistence rights for everyone, regardless of the level of economic development in a given country.

The term 'available resources' applies both to domestic resources and to any international economic or technical assistance or cooperation available to a State party. In the use of available resources, due priority should be given to the realisation of rights recognised in the Covenant, considering the need to assure to everyone the satisfaction of subsistence requirements, as well as the provision of essential services.

Importantly, the grounds of discrimination mentioned in this provision are not exhaustive and thus certain other forms of unfair discrimination negatively affecting the enjoyment of the rights enunciated in the Covenant (for instance, on the basis of sexual orientation) must be prevented.

According to the Limburg Principles, special measures taken for the sole purpose of securing adequate advancement of certain groups or individuals requiring protection in order to ensure their equal enjoyment of economic, social and cultural rights are not considered discrimination, provided that such measures do not lead to the maintenance of separate rights for different groups and are not continued after their objectives have been achieved. This applies, for example, to affirmative-action programme.

This provision not only obliges governments to desist from discriminatory behaviour and to alter laws and practices which allow discrimination, it also applies to the duty of States parties to prohibit private persons and bodies (third parties) from practising discrimination in any field of public life.

Equal Rights for Men and Women

Article 3

The States parties to the present Covenant undertake to ensure the equal right of men and women to the enjoyment of all economic, social and cultural rights set forth in the present Covenant.

Women often suffer substantial and disproportionate difficulties in securing human rights, including economic, social and cultural rights. Article 3 guarantees that men and women possess precisely the same legal entitlement to the rights set forth in the Covenant and that, if necessary, special measures will be employed by States parties to ensure that this position of equality is attained.

The Covenant provides a framework for instigating progressive and immediate measures such that women may enjoy on an equal footing rights which have often been denied them. For instance, the housing rights provisions in article 11, paragraph 1, of the Covenant must apply to men and women equally, and thus women must be accorded equal rights to housing inheritance—something which is still not the case in many countries. Together, article 3 and article 2, paragraph 2, thus provide significant legal protection against all forms of discrimination in the pursuit of economic, social and cultural rights.

Limitations

Article 4

The States parties to the present Covenant recognise that, in the enjoyment of those rights provided by the State in conformity with the present Covenant, the State may subject such rights only to such limitations as are determined by law only in so far as this may be compatible with the nature of these rights and solely for the purpose of promoting the general welfare in a democratic society.

Article 5

1. Nothing, in the present Covenant may be interpreted as implying for any State group or person any right to engage in any activity or to perform any act aimed at the destruction of any of the rights or freedoms recognised herein, or at their limitation to a greater extent than is provided for in the present Covenant.
2. No restriction upon or derogation from any of the fundamental human rights recognised or existing in any country in virtue of law, conventions, regulations or custom shall be admitted on the pretext that the present Covenant does not recognise such rights or that it recognises them to a lesser extent.

Articles 4 and 5 were not intended by the drafters of the Covenant to be overly permissive of the imposition of limitations by the state on the rights provided for. Rather, these provisions are formulated in such a manner as to be protective of the rights of individuals. They are also not designed to introduce limitations on rights affecting the subsistence or survival of the individual or the integrity of the person.

If a State party finds it necessary to invoke the provisions of these articles, it may do so only if this is provided for by law and only if the measures in question are consistent with the Covenant. Such measures cannot be applied in an arbitrary, unreasonable or discriminatory way. Moreover, individuals should have legal safeguards and effective remedies against illegal or abusive imposition of limitations on economic, social and cultural rights.

The term 'democratic society' (art. 4) further restricts the imposition of limitations under the Covenant and thus the burden rests on the State to prove that any limitations do not impair the democratic functioning of society.

None of the provisions in the law relating to any limitation may be interpreted in such a way as to nullify any of the rights or freedoms recognised in the Covenant. The main purpose of article 5, paragraph 2, is to ensure that no provision of the Covenant is interpreted so as to prejudice provisions of domestic law or any other legal instrument already in force, or which may come into force, under which more favourable treatment would be accorded to persons protected.

The Right to Work

Article 6

1. The States parties to the present Covenant recognise the right to work, which includes the right of everyone to the opportunity to gain his living by work which he freely chooses or accepts, and will take appropriate steps to safeguard this right.
2. The steps to be taken by a State party to the present Covenant to achieve the full realisation of this right shall include technical and vocational guidance and training programmes, policies and techniques to achieve steady economic, social and cultural development and full and productive employment under conditions safeguarding, fundamental political and economic freedoms to the individual.

Freely chosen work remains an essential part of being human. For many people, whether employed in the formal or informal sectors, work represents the primary source of income on which subsistence, survival and life depend. The right to work is fundamental to the enjoyment of certain subsistence and livelihood rights such as food, clothing, housing, etc. Moreover, one's working status may easily affect the enjoyment of other rights relating to health and education. The right to work is increasingly important as governments the world over continue to withdraw from the provision of basic services, leaving these to market forces and non-governmental actors.

The right to work is fundamental to ensuring the dignity and self-respect of the beneficiaries of the rights contained in the Covenant. Article 6 obliges States parties to refrain from instigating or allowing forced labour. The Committee on Economic, Social and Cultural Rights has examined this article in terms of the implementation of policies and measures aimed at securing work for all who are available to work. This right encompasses, therefore, both the right to enter into employment and the right not to be unjustly deprived of work. Although unemployment persists in all States parties, these States must apply the basic principles set out in article 2 for ensuring the full realisation of the right to work.

The Right to Just and Favourable Conditions of Work

Article 7

The States parties to the present Covenant recognise the right of everyone to the enjoyment of just and favourable conditions of work which ensure, in particular:

a) Remuneration which provides all workers, as a minimum, with:

   i) Fair wages and equal remuneration for work of equal value without distinction of any kind, in particular women being guaranteed conditions of work not inferior to those enjoyed by men, with equal pay for equal work;

ii) A decent living for themselves and their families in accordance with the provisions of the present Covenant.

b) Safe and healthy working, conditions;

c) Equal opportunity for everyone to be promoted in his employment to an appropriate higher level, subject to no considerations other than those of seniority and competence;

d) Rest, leisure and reasonable limitation of working hours and periodic holidays with pay, as well as remuneration for public holidays.

Article 7 establishes a right to a minimum remuneration for employment, stipulating fair wages sufficient to guarantee a decent living, as well as working conditions that are just and favourable. Wages must be equitable and just in order to be considered fair.

This article relates closely to a large number of conventions adopted by the International Labour Organisation, including the Minimum Wage Fixing Convention (No. 131, 1970) and the Equal Remuneration Convention (No. 100, 1951).

People must be afforded minimum conditions of occupational health and safety, and States parties are responsible for adopting policies and laws to that end. A coherent national policy in this regard is incumbent on all States parties.

The standards laid down in article 7 also relate to the duties of States parties to reduce the working week in a progressive manner and to ensure that workers enjoy adequate rest and holidays. For all aspects of this article, States parties must establish a baseline or minimum standard below which the working conditions of no worker should be allowed to fall; they must also develop enforcement measures guaranteeing these rights.

The Right to Form and Join Trade Unions

Article 8

1. The States Parties to the present Covenant undertake to ensure:

   a) The right of everyone to form trade unions and join the trade union of his choice, subject only to the rules of the organisation concerned, for the promotion and protection of his economic and social interests. No restrictions may be placed on the exercise of this right other than those prescribed by law and which are necessary in a democratic society in the interests of national security or public order or for the protection of the rights and freedoms of others;

   b) The right of trade unions to establish national federations or confederations and the right of the latter to form or join international trade-union organisations;

   c) The right of trade unions to function freely subject to no limitations other than those prescribed by law and which are necessary in a democratic society in the interests of national security or public order or for the protection of the rights and freedoms of others;

d) The right to strike, provided that it is exercised in conformity with the laws of the particular country.

2. This article shall not prevent the imposition of lawful restrictions on the exercise of these rights by members of the armed forces or of the police or of the administration of the State.

3. Nothing in this article shall authorise States parties to the International Labour Organisation Convention of 1948 concerning Freedom of Association and Protection of the Right to Organise to take legislative measures which would prejudice, or apply the law in such a manner as would prejudice, the guarantees provided for in that Convention.

The right to form and join trade unions is closely linked to the right to freedom of association, which is widely recognised throughout international human rights law. These rights, combined with the right to strike, are fundamental if the rights of workers and other citizens under the Covenant are to be implemented.

Article 8 provides for a right not to be compelled to join a particular trade union, in accordance with the term 'of his choice' (para. 1(a)). It also includes the right to federate or confederate, which should not be subject to state control. The right to collective bargaining, the right to protection from dissolution or suspension and the right to strike are also protected.

States parties are allowed some measure of discretion concerning the implementation of article 8, as evidenced by the language concerning limitations in the interests of national security, public order and the rights and freedoms of others. These grounds for exemption, however, must be interpreted narrowly by States parties seeking to invoke them.

With regard to national security concerns, for instance, the Limburg Principles on the Implementation of the International Covenant on Economic, Social and Cultural Rights stress that the systematic violation of economic, social and cultural rights undermines true national security and may jeopardise international peace and security. A State responsible for such violation shall not invoke national security as a justification for measures aimed at suppressing opposition to such violation or at perpetrating repressive practices against its population.

The Right to Social Security and Social Insurance

Article 9

The States parties to the present Covenant recognise the right of everyone to social security, including social insurance.

A large number of States do not maintain adequate social security or social insurance provisions under domestic laws protecting people in circumstances such as old age, disability, ill-health or other situations not allowing them to earn a decent living. At the same time, many countries which do provide such protection are beginning to transfer responsibility for these matters from the state to the private sector. These issues raise serious concerns regarding enjoyment of the rights contained in the Covenant.

The Committee on Economic, Social and Cultural Rights specifically asks States parties whether they maintain social security schemes in the following areas: medical care, cash sickness benefits, maternity benefits, old-age benefits, invalidity benefits, survivors' benefits, employment injury benefits, unemployment benefits and family benefits.

The Committee has devoted particular attention to enjoyment of the rights provided for in article 9 by women, older persons (General Comment No. 6 (1995)), and persons with disabilities (General Comment No. 5 (1994)).

Protection and Assistance for the Family

Article 10

The States parties to the Present Covenant recognise that:

1. The widest possible protection and assistance should be accorded to the family, which is the natural and fundamental group unit of society, particularly for its establishment and while it is responsible for the care and education of dependent children. Marriage must be entered into with the free consent of the intending spouses.

2. Special protection should be accorded to mothers during a reasonable period before and after childbirth. During such period working mothers should be accorded paid leave or leave with adequate social security benefits.

3. Special measures of protection and assistance should be taken on behalf of all children and young persons without any discrimination for reasons of parentage or other conditions. Children and young persons should be protected from economic and social exploitation. Their employment in work harmful to their morals or health or dangerous to life or likely to hamper their normal development should be

punishable by law. States should also set age limits below which the paid employment of child labour should be prohibited and punishable by law.

Article 10 provides protection for the family, mothers and children. It includes the right to enter freely into marriage, raising doubts as to the situation in countries where marriage occurs without the free and informed consent of one or another spouse, almost invariably the woman. Mothers are to be accorded substantial protection before and after childbirth. The Committee on Economic, Social and Cultural Rights regularly requests information from States parties as to whether any particular groups of women lack such protection.

The Committee has not spent a great deal of time examining situations relating to family rights, but has devoted increased attention to the rights of the child as they are established under article 10, paragraph 3. It has paid particular attention to child labour and the living conditions of children. The most intensive work within the United Nations system on children's rights is carried out by the Committee on the Rights of the Child, with which the Committee on Economic, Social and Cultural Rights works closely.

The Right to an Adequate Standard of Living

Article 11

1. The States parties to the present Covenant recognise the right of everyone to an adequate standard of living for himself and his family, including adequate food, clothing and housing, and to the continuous improvement of living conditions. The States parties will take appropriate steps to ensure the realisation of

this right, recognising to this effect the essential importance of international cooperation based on free consent.

2. The States parties to the present Covenant, recognising the fundamental right of everyone to be free from hunger, shall take, individually and through international cooperation, the measures, including specific programmes, which are needed :

   a) To improve methods of production, conservation and distribution of food by making full use of technical and scientific knowledge, by disseminating knowledge of the principles of nutrition and by developing or reforming agrarian systems in such a way as to achieve the most efficient development and utilisation of natural resources;

   b) Taking into account the problems of both food-importing and food-exporting countries, to ensure an equitable distribution of world food supplies in relation to need.

Article 11 incorporates a broad range of concerns relating to the lives and livelihoods of residents of States parties, in particular food, clothing and housing. The Committee on Economic, Social and Cultural Rights has devoted extensive attention to this article, particularly as it relates to the human right to adequate housing. To date, the right to adequate housing is the only right in the Covenant which has had an entire general comment devoted to it (General Comment No. 4 (1991)).

General Comment No. 4 reveals the extensive nature of the protection included under article 11 and elaborates legal interpretations of the right to adequate housing which go far beyond restricted visions of this right as simply a right to shelter. In it, the Committee, which has given more attention to the right to housing than to any other right under the Covenant, states :

> . . . the right to housing, should not be interpreted in a narrower restrictive sense which equates it with, for example, the shelter provided by merely having a roof over one's head . . . Rather it should be seen as the right to live somewhere in security, peace and dignity . . . . (Para. 7.)

The Committee has defined the term 'adequate housing' to comprise security of tenure, availability of services, affordability, habitability, accessibility, location and cultural adequacy.

Article 11 does not imply a stagnant state of affairs, but also includes a right 'to the continuous improvement of living conditions' (para. 1) and the possibilities associated with international cooperation in the event of States parties being unable to guarantee the rights in question. This is particularly relevant in times of food crises or famine.

The Committee has decided on several occasions that certain States parties had violated provisions of article 11, particularly as a result of the practice of forced evictions. This is indicative of the seriousness which the Committee accords article 11.

The Right to the Highest Attainable Standard of Physical and Mental Health

Article 12

1. The States parties to the present Covenant recognise the right of everyone to the enjoyment of the highest attainable standard of physical and mental health.

2. The steps to be taken by the States parties to the present Covenant to achieve the full realisation of this right shall include those necessary for:

   a) The provision for the reduction of the stillbirth-rate and of infant mortality and for the healthy development of the child;

   b) The improvement of all aspects of environmental and industrial hygiene;

   c) The prevention, treatment and control of epidemic, endemic, occupational and other diseases;

   d) The creation of conditions which would assure to all medical service and medical attention in the event of sickness.

Recognition of the right to health obviously does not mean that beneficiaries of this right have a right to be healthy. Rather, the Covenant stresses the obligation of States parties to ensure for their citizens "the highest attainable standard of . . . health".

Article 12 therefore places emphasis on equal access to health care and minimum guarantees of health care in the event of sickness.

The Committee on Economic, Social and Cultural Rights has spent increasing energy on clarifying and monitoring health rights, having held a general discussion on the topic and adopted a general comment on the rights of persons with disabilities (General Comment No. 5 (1994)). The rights of people with HIV/AIDS have also received increasing attention from the Committee in recent years.

The Right to Education

Article 13

1. The States parties to the present Covenant recognise the right of everyone to education. They agree that education shall be directed to the full development of the human personality and the sense of its dignity, and shall strengthen the respect for human rights and fundamental freedoms. They further agree that education shall enable all persons to participate effectively in a free society, promote understanding, tolerance and friendship among all nations and all racial, ethnic or religious groups, and further the activities of the United Nations for the maintenance of peace.

2. The States parties to the present Covenant recognise that, with a view to achieving the full realisation of this right:

   a) Primary education shall be compulsory and available free to all;

   b) Secondary education in its different forms, including technical and vocational secondary education, shall be made generally available and accessible to all by every appropriate means, and in particular by the progressive introduction of free education;

   c) Higher education shall be made equally accessible to all, on the basis of capacity, by every appropriate means, and in particular by the progressive introduction of free education;

   d) Fundamental education shall be encouraged or intensified as far as possible for those persons who have not received or completed the whole period of their primary education;

e) The development of a system of schools at all levels shall be actively pursued, an adequate fellowship system shall be established, and the material conditions of teaching staff shall be continuously improved.

3. The States parties to the present Covenant undertake to have respect for the liberty of parents and, when applicable, legal guardians to choose for their children schools, other than those established by the public authorities, which conform to such minimum educational standards as may be laid down or approved by the State and to ensure the religious and moral education of their children in conformity with their own convictions.

4. No part of this article shall be construed so as to interfere with the liberty of individuals and bodies to establish and direct educational institutions, subject always to the observance of the principles set forth in paragraph one of this article and to the requirement that the education given in such institutions shall conform to such minimum standards as may be laid down by the State.

Compulsory and Free Primary Education

Article 14

Each State party to the present Covenant which, at the time of becoming a Party, has not been able to secure in its metropolitan territory or other territories under its jurisdiction compulsory primary education, free of charge, undertakes within two years, to work out and adopt a detailed plan of action for the progressive implementation, within a reasonable number of years, to be fixed in the plan, of the principle of compulsory education free of charge for all.

Articles 13 and 14 recognise that education is a fundamental precondition for the enjoyment and assertion of human rights and that education strengthens human rights and basic democratic principles. The international community has long recognised these basic truths and has proclaimed the decade 1995-2004 as the United Nations Decade for Human Rights Education. The Committee on Economic, Social and Cultural Rights held a general discussion on this topic in 1994.

These two articles guarantee all children a right to free and compulsory primary education, wherever they may live. They also enshrine the right to equal access to education and equal enjoyment of education facilities; the freedom to choose education and to establish educational institutions; the protection of pupils against inhuman disciplinary measures and academic freedom.

The Right to Culture and to Benefit from Scientific Progress

Article 15

1. The States parties to the present Covenant recognise the right of everyone:

   a) To take part in cultural life;

   b) To enjoy the benefits of scientific progress and its applications;

c) To benefit from the protection of the moral and material interests resulting from any scientific, literary or artistic production of which he is the author.

2. The steps to be taken by the States parties to the present Covenant to achieve the full realisation of this right shall include those necessary for the conservation, the development and the diffusion of science and culture.

3. The States parties to the present Covenant undertake to respect the freedom indispensable for scientific research and creative activity.

4. The States parties to the present Covenant recognise the benefits to be derived from the encouragement and development of international contacts and cooperation in the scientific and cultural fields.

The rights to enjoy culture, to participate in cultural life and to benefit from technological and scientific progress form the foundation of article 15. Although these issues may not seem to be matters of human rights, they are of fundamental importance to the principles of equality of treatment, freedom of expression, the right to receive and impart information, and the right to the full development of the human personality.

Cultural attributes can often be attacked or derided by States in attempts to favour one national, racial or ethnic group over another, to cite but one example of how important the rights in question are. Moreover, these rights include the right to participate in the life of society, giving a wide reading to the term 'culture'.

The right to benefit from scientific progress and its applications is designed to ensure that everyone in society can enjoy advances in this regard, in particular disadvantaged groups. It includes the right of everyone to seek and receive information about such advances resulting from new scientific insights and to have access to any developments which could enhance their enjoyment of the rights contained in the Covenant.

Vienna Declaration and Programme of Action

Although the Committee on Economic, Social and Cultural Rights can assist in the implementation of the Covenant from an international perspective, the ultimate effectiveness of this instrument is contingent on the measures taken by governments to give actual effect to their international legal obligations. In this regard, the Committee has recognised the essential importance of the adoption by States of appropriate legislative measures and the provision of judicial remedies, indicating the very real legal nature of economic, social and cultural rights.

The necessity of implementing the provisions of the Covenant through domestic legislation is consistent with article 27 of the 1969 Vienna Convention on the Law of Treaties, which states that "a party may not invoke the provisions of its internal law as justification for its failure to perform a treaty." Indeed, the Covenant often requires legislative action to be taken in cases where existing legislation is in violation of the obligations assumed under the Covenant.

The Limburg Principles on the Implementation of the International Covenant on Economic, Social and Cultural Rights emphasise that "States parties shall provide for effective remedies, including, where appropriate, judicial remedies" (Principle 19). Because there does not yet exist an individual complaints procedure under the Covenant, the full implementation of the rights which this instrument contains is all the more dependent on the provision of appropriate laws and remedies at the national level.

At minimum, the national and local judiciaries of States parties must consider international human rights laws such as the Covenant an interpretative aid to domestic law and ensure that domestic law is interpreted and applied in a manner consistent with the provisions of international human rights instruments ratified by the State. From the perspective of international law, the underlying principle is that courts should avoid placing their government in violation of the terms of an international treaty which it has ratified.

Regarding the justifiability of the rights contained in the Covenant—i.e., the possibility of their being subjected to judicial review—the Committee has stated in its General Comment No. 3 (1990):

> Among, the measures which might be considered appropriate, in addition to legislation, is the provision of judicial remedies with respect to rights which may, in accordance with the national legal system, be considered justifiable . . . (Para. 5.)

In this regard, the Committee has indicated that a number of articles in the Covenant are capable of immediate implementation, including article 3, article 7, subparagraph (a) (i), article 8, article 10, paragraph 3, article 13, paragraphs 2 (a), 3 and 4, and article 15, paragraph 3. It has also stressed, with respect to the right to adequate housing, for example, that "instances of forced eviction are *prima facie* incompatible with the requirements of the Covenant and can only be justified in the most exceptional circumstances, and in accordance with the relevant principles of international law." In order to put such obligations into effect domestically, national courts would obviously have an important role to play in ensuring respect for the rights in question.

Monitoring the Implementation of the Covenant: the Committee on Economic, Social and Cultural Rights

Creation and Composition of the Committee

Unlike the five other human rights treaty bodies, the Committee on Economic, Social and Cultural Rights was not established by its corresponding instrument. Rather, the Economic and Social Council (ECOSOC) created the Committee, following the less than ideal performance of two previous bodies entrusted with monitoring the Covenant.

The Committee was established in 1985, met for the first time in 1987 and has to date held 14 sessions. Meeting initially on an annual basis, the Committee currently convenes twice a year, holding two three-week sessions, generally in May and November/December. It holds all its meetings at the United Nations Office at Geneva.

The Committee comprise 18 members who are experts with recognised competence in the field of human rights. Members of the Committee are independent and serve in their personal capacity, not as representatives of Governments. At present, the Committee is made up of 13 men and five women. The Committee itself selects its chairperson, three vice-chairpersons and rapporteur.

Members of the Committee are elected by ECOSOC for four-year terms, and are eligible for re-election if renominated. The Committee is thus a subsidiary organ of ECOSOC and derives its formal authority from that body. Elections take place in a secret ballot from a list of nominees proposed by States parties to the Covenant. States which have not ratified the Covenant cannot, therefore, nominate their own nationals for positions on the Committee. The principles of equitable geographical distribution and the representation of different social and legal systems guide the selection process. The Committee is serviced by the United Nations Centre for Human Rights.

The primary function of the Committee is to monitor the implementation of the Covenant by States parties. It strives to develop a constructive dialogue with States parties and seeks to determine through a variety of means whether or not the norms contained in the Covenant are being adequately applied in States parties and how the implementation and enforcement of the Covenant could be improved so that all people who are entitled to the rights enshrined in the Covenant can actually enjoy them in full.

Drawing on the legal and practical expertise of its members, the Committee can also assist governments in fulfilling their obligations under the Covenant by issuing specific legislative, policy and other suggestions and recommendations such that economic, social and cultural rights are more effectively secured.

How do States Parties Report to the Committee?

Under articles 16 and 17 of the Covenant, States parties undertake to submit periodic reports to the Committee-within two years of the entry into force of the Covenant for a particular State party, and thereafter once every five years—outlining the legislative, judicial, policy and other measures which they have taken to ensure the enjoyment of the rights contained in the Covenant. States parties are also requested to provide detailed data on the degree to which the rights are implemented and areas where particular difficulties have been faced in this respect.

The Committee has assisted the reporting process by providing States parties with a detailed 22-page set of reporting guidelines specifying the types of information the Committee requires in order to monitor compliance with the Covenant effectively.

The reporting requirement is much more than simply a formalistic commitment. Although the reporting process is imbued with a number of difficulties, not the least of which are the non-submission of reports by a large number of States parties and problems relating to resource constraints of States, this mechanism has a number of important functions. Among these are the initial review function, the monitoring function, the policy formulation function, the public scrutiny function, the evaluation function, the function of acknowledging problems and the information-exchange function.

The Committee has emphasised that reporting obligations under the Covenant fulfil seven key objectives. In its General Comment No. 1 (1989), the Committee stated these objectives as follows:

1. to ensure that a State party undertakes a comprehensive review of national legislation, administrative rules and procedures, and practices in order to assure the fullest possible conformity with the Covenant;

2. to ensure that the State party regularly monitors the actual situation with respect to each of the enumerated rights in order to assess the extent to which the various rights are being enjoyed by all individuals within the country;

3. to provide a basis for government elaboration of clearly stated and carefully targeted policies for implementing the Covenant;

4. to facilitate public scrutiny of government policies with respect to the Covenant's implementation, and to encourage the involvement of the various sectors of society in the formulation, implementation and review of relevant policies;

5. to provide a basis on which both the State party and the Committee can effectively evaluate progress towards the realisation of the obligations contained in the Covenant;

6. to enable the State party to develop a better understanding of problems and shortcomings impeding the realisation of economic, social and cultural rights;

7. to facilitate the exchange of information among States parties and to help develop a fuller appreciation of both common problems and possible solutions in the realisation of each of the rights contained in the Covenant.

The Committee typically considers some five or six reports of States parties during any given session. If a State party which has submitted a report that is scheduled for the Committee's consideration at a given session seeks to defer the presentation of the report at the last minute, the Committee does not grant such a request, and proceeds with its consideration, even in the absence of a State party representative.

The Committee has also had to grapple with problems relating to the non-submission of reports and reports which are considerably overdue. In response to such situations, the Committee has notified States parties whose reports are long overdue of its intention to consider these reports at specified future sessions. If no report is forthcoming, the Committee then proceeds to consider the status of economic, social and cultural rights in the States concerned in the light of all available information.

Submission of Reports and the Pre-sessional Working Group

When States parties submit their reports, a standard procedure of consideration is followed by the Committee. Once received, processed and translated by the Secretariat, States parties' reports are initially reviewed by the Committee's five-person pre-sessional working group, which meets six months prior to a report being considered by the full Committee. The pre-sessional working group gives a preliminary consideration to the report, appoints one member to give particular consideration to each report, and develops written lists of questions based on disparities found in the reports which are submitted to the States parties concerned. The States parties are then required to reply in writing to these questions prior to their appearance before the Committee.

Presentation of Reports

Representatives of reporting States are strongly encouraged to be present at meetings when the

Committee considers their reports. Such delegations are virtually always present during this process, which is generally carried out over a two-day period. Delegations first provide introductory comments and responses to the pre-sessional working group's written questions. This is followed by the provision of information by the United Nations specialised agencies relevant to the report under consideration. Committee members then put questions and observations to the State party appearing before it. A further period of time is then allowed for representatives of States parties to respond, generally not on the same day, to the questions and views put to them, as precisely as possible. If the questions cannot be adequately dealt with, the Committee often requests a State party to provide it with additional information for its consideration at forthcoming sessions.

Concluding Observations: The Committee Decides

Upon completion by the Committee of its analysis of reports and the appearance by States parties, the Committee concludes its consideration of States parties' reports by issuing 'concluding observations', which constitute the decision of the Committee regarding the status of the Covenant in a given State party. Concluding observations are divided into five sections: (a) introduction; (b) positive aspects; (c) factors and difficulties impeding the implementation of the Covenant; (d) principal subjects of concern; and (e) suggestions and recommendations. Concluding observations are adopted in private session, and are released to the public on the final day of each session.

On a number of occasions, the Committee has concluded that violations of the Covenant had taken place, and subsequently urged States parties to desist from any further infringements of the rights in question.

All human rights are subject to violation, and economic, social and cultural rights are no exception. The Limburg Principles on the Implementation of the International Covenant on Economic, Social and Cultural Rights list the following circumstances amounting to violations of the Covenant by a State party (principle 72): (a) it fails to take a step which the Covenant requires it to take; (b) it fails to remove promptly obstacles which it is obligated to remove to permit the immediate fulfilment of a right; (c) it fails to implement without delay a right which the Covenant requires it to provide immediately; (d) it wilfully fails to meet a generally accepted international minimum standard of achievement, which is within its powers to meet; (e) it applies a limitation to a right recognised in the Covenant in a manner not in accordance with the Covenant; (f) it deliberately retards or halts the progressive realisation of a right, unless it is acting within a limitation permitted by the Covenant or it does so because of a lack of available resources; and (g) it fails to submit reports as required under the Covenant.

While the Committee's concluding observations, in particular suggestions and recommendations, may not carry legally binding status, they are indicative of the opinion of the only expert body entrusted with and capable of making such pronouncements. Consequently, for States parties to ignore or not act on such views would be to show bad faith in implementing their Covenant-based obligations. In a number of instances, changes in policy, practice and law have been registered at least partly in response to the Committee's concluding observations.

In addition to concluding observations, letters from the chairperson are occasionally addressed to States parties informing them of the Committee's concerns.

The Committee also adopts draft decisions for eventual adoption by ECOSOC, when such approval is required. This is generally the case when the Committee requests a State party to issue it with an invitation to visit the country and provide the government with technical and other assistance which it may require in order to implement more fully and enforce the norms of the Covenant. The Committee has to date twice requested invitations to visit the territories of States parties (Dominican Republic and Panama). Only in one of these instances (Panama), however, did the State issue the requisite invitation, and a mission took place in April 1995.

Generating Interpretative Clarity

a) General Comments

The Committee decided in 1988 to begin preparing 'general comments' on the rights and provisions contained in the Covenant with a view to assisting States parties in fulfilling their reporting obligations and to provide greater interpretative clarity as to the intent, meaning and content of the Covenant. The Committee further views the adoption of general comments as a means of promoting the implementation of the Covenant, by drawing the attention of States parties to insufficiencies disclosed by a large number of States parties' reports, and by inducing renewed attention to particular provisions of the Covenant on the part of States parties, United Nations agencies and others with a view to achieving progressively the full realisation of the rights established under the Covenant.

General comments are a crucial means of generating jurisprudence, providing a method by which members of the Committee may come to an agreement by consensus regarding the interpretation of norms embodied in the Covenant.

As of April 1996, the Committee has adopted six general comments. These are:

— General Comment No. 1 (1989) on reporting by States parties;

— General Comment No. 2 (1990) on international technical assistance measures (art. 22);

— General Comment No. 3 (1990) on the nature of States parties' obligations (art. 2, para. 1, of the Covenant);

— General Comment No. 4 (1991) on the right to adequate housing (art. 11, para. 1, of the Covenant);

— General Comment No. 5 (1994) on persons with disabilities;

— General Comment No. 6 (1995) on the economic, social and cultural rights of older persons.

It is likely that the Committee will consider the adoption of additional general comments in the near future on issues such as the right to health; the domestic application of the Covenant; forced evictions and the Covenant; the non-discrimination clauses of the Covenant (art. 2, para. 2); the right to food; and others.

b) General Discussions

At each of its sessions, the Committee holds a 'day of general discussion' on particular provisions of the Covenant, particular human rights or other themes of direct relevance to the Committee in order to develop its understanding of the issues concerned. The Committee has sought to draw on a wide range of expertise during these discussions and has, therefore, engaged in dialogue with United Nations special rapporteurs, experts from relevant non-governmental organisations and representatives of United Nations specialised agencies.

General discussions to date have been held on the right to food (1989); the right to housing (1990); economic and social indicators (1991); the right to take part in cultural life (1992); the rights of the ageing and elderly (1993); the right to health (1993); the role of social safety nets as a means of protecting economic, social and cultural rights, with particular reference to situations involving major structural adjustment and/or transition to a free market economy (1994); human rights education (1994); the interpretation and practical application of the obligations incumbent on States parties (1995); and a draft optional protocol to the Covenant (1995).

Civil Society and the Work of the Committee

The World Conference on Human Rights affirms that extreme poverty and social exclusion constitute a violation of human dignity and that urgent steps are necessary to achieve better knowledge of extreme poverty and its causes, including those related to the problem of development, in order to promote the human rights of the poorest, and to put an end to extreme poverty and social exclusion and to promote the enjoyment of the fruits of social progress. It is essential for States to foster participation by the poorest people in the decision-making process and the community in which they live, the promotion of human rights and efforts to combat extreme poverty.

Relevance of NGOs and CBOs

The Committee has long recognised the important contribution which can be made by civil society in the provision of information concerning the status of the Covenant within States parties. The Committee was the first treaty body to provide non-governmental organisations (NGOs) with the opportunity to submit written statements and make oral submissions dealing with issues relating to the enjoyment or non-enjoyment of the rights contained in the Covenant in specific countries.

On the first day of each session of the Committee, the afternoon meeting is set aside to give international and national NGOs and community-based organisations (CBOs) an opportunity to express their views about how the Covenant is or is not implemented by States parties. The Committee will receive oral testimony from NGOs as long as the information focuses specifically on the provisions of the Covenant, is of direct relevance to matters under consideration by the Committee, is reliable and is not abusive. In recent years, NGOs and CBOs have taken increased advantage of this procedure and provided the Committee with written, audio and video materials alleging the non-enjoyment of economic, social and cultural rights in States parties.

The Committee has indicated that the purposes of the NGO procedure are to enable it to inform itself as fully as possible, to examine the accuracy and pertinence of information which would most probably be available to it anyway, and to put the process of receiving NGO information on a more transparent basis.

NGOs and CBOs wishing to provide reliable and new information to the Committee may write to the secretariat of the Committee several months prior to the beginning of a particular session, with a specific request to intervene during the NGO procedure. Groups with written materials may also send these to the secretariat, and may attend Committee sessions. NGOs in consultative status with the United Nations or other groups which have relations with such NGOs also may attend Committee sessions. NGOs with consultative status may, in accordance with the relevant ECOSOC resolutions, submit written submissions to the Committee at any time. Committee sessions are generally held in public, with the exception of meetings at which it prepares its concluding observations, which are held privately.

The active participation of NGOs in the work of the Committee has also proven fundamental in ensuring the wide distribution of information about the Covenant and the Committee at the national and local levels. In many instances, these organisations have generated substantial media attention in their countries following the adoption of concluding observations regarding the States in question.

Towards a Formal Complaints Procedure (Optional Protocol)

At present it is not possible for individuals or groups who feel that their rights under the Covenant have been violated to submit formal complaints to the Committee. The absence of such procedure places significant constraints on the ability of the Committee to develop jurisprudence or case-law and, of course, greatly limits the chances of victims of abuses of the Covenant obtaining international redress.

There are numerous arguments supporting the adoption of a complaints procedure under the Covenant. These include the improved enjoyment by people of economic, social and cultural rights; a strengthening of international accountability of States parties; increased congruence in the legal standing and seriousness accorded to both International Covenants; a refinement of the rights and duties emerging from the provisions of the International Covenant on Economic, Social and Cultural Rights; and a structural and concrete affirmation of the indivisibility and interdependence of all human rights. It is also argued that such a procedure would encourage States parties to provide similar remedies at the local and national levels.

The Committee has devoted increasing attention to the possibility of elaborating such an optional protocol since 1990 and has discussed the issue at length on several occasions. (20) At its sixth session, in 1991, the Committee supported the drafting of an optional protocol "since that would enhance the practical implementation of the Covenant as well as the dialogue with States parties and would make it possible to focus the attention of public opinion to a greater extent on economic, social and cultural rights."

The World Conference on Human Rights, held at Vienna in June 1993, gave added impetus to this initiative by asserting, in the Vienna Declaration and Programme of Action which it adopted, that the Committee should continue its efforts towards this end. The Committee has prepared a draft optional protocol, but it has yet to be officially adopted by the relevant United Nations organs.

Many other initiatives have also addressed the desirability of including a complaints procedure under the International Covenant on economic, Social and Cultural Rights, and these have given added support to this means of strengthening this pivotal human rights treaty.

Pending the addition of an optional protocol, beneficiaries of the rights contained in the Covenant may still have recourse to the general procedures of the Committee, and may utilise what has been called an unofficial petition procedure" based on the modalities of the Committee.

NGO Participation in the Activities of the Committee on Economic, Social and Cultural Rights

At its eighth session, in May 1993, the Committee adopted the following procedure regarding the participation of non-governmental organisations in its activities:

A. Written Information

1. The Committee reiterates its long-standing invitation to NGOs to submit to it in writing, at any time, information regarding any aspect of its work.

B. Oral Information

2. In addition to the receipt of written information, a short period of time will be made available at the

beginning of each session of the pre-sessional working group to provide NGOs with an opportunity to submit relevant oral information to the members of the working group.

3. Furthermore, the Committee will set aside part of the first afternoon at each of its sessions to enable it to receive oral information provided by NGOs. Such information should: (a) focus specifically on the provisions of the International Covenant on Economic, Social and Cultural Rights; (b) be of direct relevance to matters under consideration by the Committee; (c) be reliable; (d) not be abusive. The relevant meeting, will be open and will be provided with interpretation services, but will not be covered by summary records. The purposes are: to enable the Committee to inform itself as fully as possible; to probe the accuracy and pertinence of information which would most probably be available to it anyway; and to put the process of receiving NGO information on a more transparent and open basis than is permitted by the current approach.

4. NGOs wishing to present oral information should inform the Committee in advance. In cases in which the Committee receives more expressions of interest than can be dealt with in the limited time available, the Chairperson of the Committee, in consultation with the Bureau, shall determine on an objective basis which NGOs will be invited to make an oral presentation.

5. To the extent that information provided to the Committee in writing, under these procedures is referred to by any member of the Committee in questions posed to the State party, the relevant

information should be available for consultation by the government concerned and all other interested parties.

6. The Committee requests its Chairperson, in conjunction with the secretariat, to make these procedures as widely known as possible.

5

International Covenant on Civil and Political Rights

(Adopted by General Assembly resolution 2200A (XXI) of 16 December 1966)

Preamble

The States Parties to the present Covenant,

Considering that, in accordance with the principles proclaimed in the Charter of the United Nations, recognition of the inherent dignity and of the equal and inalienable rights of all members of the human family is the foundation of freedom, justice and peace in the world,

Recognizing that these rights derive from the inherent dignity of the human person,

Recognizing that, in accordance with the Universal Declaration of Human Rights, the ideal of free human beings enjoying civil and political freedom and freedom from fear and want can only be achieved if conditions are created whereby everyone may enjoy his civil and political rights, as well as his economic, social and cultural rights,

Considering the obligation of States under the Charter of the United Nations to promote universal respect for, and observance of, human rights and freedoms,

Realizing that the individual, having duties to other individuals and to the community to which he belongs, is under a responsibility to strive for the promotion and observance of the rights recognized in the present Covenant,

Agree upon the following articles:

PART I

Article 1 General comment on its implementation

1. All peoples have the right of self-determination. By virtue of that right they freely determine their political status and freely pursue their economic, social and cultural development.
2. All peoples may, for their own ends, freely dispose of their natural wealth and resources without prejudice to any obligations arising out of international economic cooperation, based upon the principle of mutual benefit, and international law. In no case may a people be deprived of its own means of subsistence.
3. The States Parties to the present Covenant, including those having responsibility for the administration of Non-Self-Governing and Trust Territories, shall promote the realization of the right of self-

determination, and shall respect that right, in conformity with the provisions of the Charter of the United Nations.

PART II

Article 2 General comment on its implementation

1. Each State Party to the present Covenant undertakes to respect and to ensure to all individuals within its territory and subject to its jurisdiction the rights recognized in the present Covenant, without distinction of any kind, such as race, colour, sex, language, religion, political or other opinion, national or social origin, property, birth or other status.
2. Where not already provided for by existing legislative or other measures, each State Party to the present Covenant undertakes to take the necessary steps, in accordance with its constitutional processes and with the provisions of the present Covenant, to adopt such laws or other measures as may be necessary to give effect to the rights recognized in the present Covenant.
3. Each State Party to the present Covenant undertakes:
   (a) To ensure that any person whose rights or freedoms as herein recognized are violated shall have an effective remedy, notwithstanding that the violation has been committed by persons acting in an official capacity;
   (b) To ensure that any person claiming such a remedy shall have his right thereto determined

by competent judicial, administrative or legislative authorities, or by any other competent authority provided for by the legal system of the State, and to develop the possibilities of judicial remedy;

(c) To ensure that the competent authorities shall enforce such remedies when granted.

Article 3 General comment on its implementation

The States Parties to the present Covenant undertake to ensure the equal right of men and women to the enjoyment of all civil and political rights set forth in the present Covenant. General comment on its implementation

Article 4 General comment on its implementation

1. In time of public emergency which threatens the life of the nation and the existence of which is officially proclaimed, the States Parties to the present Covenant may take measures derogating from their obligations under the present Covenant to the extent strictly required by the exigencies of the situation, provided that such measures are not inconsistent with their other obligations under international law and do not involve discrimination solely on the ground of race, colour, sex, language, religion or social origin.

2. No derogation from articles 6, 7, 8 (paragraphs I and 2), 11, 15, 16 and 18 may be made under this provision.

3. Any State Party to the present Covenant availing itself of the right of derogation shall immediately inform the other States Parties to the present Covenant, through the intermediary of the Secretary-General of the United Nations, of the provisions from which it has derogated and of the reasons by which it was actuated. A further communication shall be made, through the same intermediary, on the date on which it terminates such derogation.

Article 5

1. Nothing in the present Covenant may be interpreted as implying for any State, group or person any right to engage in any activity or perform any act aimed at the destruction of any of the rights and freedoms recognized herein or at their limitation to a greater extent than is provided for in the present Covenant.
2. There shall be no restriction upon or derogation from any of the fundamental human rights recognized or existing in any State Party to the present Covenant pursuant to law, conventions, regulations or custom on the pretext that the present Covenant does not recognize such rights or that it recognizes them to a lesser extent.

PART III

Article 6 General comment on its implementation

1. Every human being has the inherent right to life. This right shall be protected by law. No one shall be arbitrarily deprived of his life.

2. In countries which have not abolished the death penalty, sentence of death may be imposed only for the most serious crimes in accordance with the law in force at the time of the commission of the crime and not contrary to the provisions of the present Covenant and to the Convention on the Prevention and Punishment of the Crime of Genocide. This penalty can only be carried out pursuant to a final judgement rendered by a competent court.
3. When deprivation of life constitutes the crime of genocide, it is understood that nothing in this article shall authorize any State Party to the present Covenant to derogate in any way from any obligation assumed under the provisions of the Convention on the Prevention and Punishment of the Crime of Genocide.
4. Anyone sentenced to death shall have the right to seek pardon or commutation of the sentence. Amnesty, pardon or commutation of the sentence of death may be granted in all cases.
5. Sentence of death shall not be imposed for crimes committed by persons below eighteen years of age and shall not be carried out on pregnant women.
6. Nothing in this article shall be invoked to delay or to prevent the abolition of capital punishment by any State Party to the present Covenant.

Article 7 General comment on its implementation

No one shall be subjected to torture or to cruel, inhuman or degrading treatment or punishment. In particular, no one shall be subjected without his free consent to medical or scientific experimentation.

Article 8

1. No one shall be held in slavery; slavery and the slave-trade in all their forms shall be prohibited.
2. No one shall be held in servitude.
3.
   (a) No one shall be required to perform forced or compulsory labour;
   (b) Paragraph 3 (a) shall not be held to preclude, in countries where imprisonment with hard labour may be imposed as a punishment for a crime, the performance of hard labour in pursuance of a sentence to such punishment by a competent court;
   (c) For the purpose of this paragraph the term "forced or compulsory labour" shall not include:
      (i) Any work or service, not referred to in subparagraph (b), normally required of a person who is under detention in consequence of a lawful order of a court, or of a person during conditional release from such detention;
      (ii) Any service of a military character and, in countries where conscientious objection is recognized, any national service required by law of conscientious objectors;
      (iii) Any service exacted in cases of emergency or calamity threatening the life or well-being of the community;
      (iv) Any work or service which forms part of normal civil obligations.

Article 9 General comment on its implementation

1. Everyone has the right to liberty and security of person. No one shall be subjected to arbitrary arrest or detention. No one shall be deprived of his liberty except on such grounds and in accordance with such procedure as are established by law.

2. Anyone who is arrested shall be informed, at the time of arrest, of the reasons for his arrest and shall be promptly informed of any charges against him.

3. Anyone arrested or detained on a criminal charge shall be brought promptly before a judge or other officer authorized by law to exercise judicial power and shall be entitled to trial within a reasonable time or to release. It shall not be the general rule that persons awaiting trial shall be detained in custody, but release may be subject to guarantees to appear for trial, at any other stage of the judicial proceedings, and, should occasion arise, for execution of the judgement.

4. Anyone who is deprived of his liberty by arrest or detention shall be entitled to take proceedings before a court, in order that court may decide without delay on the lawfulness of his detention and order his release if the detention is not lawful.

5. Anyone who has been the victim of unlawful arrest or detention shall have an enforceable right to compensation.

Article 10 General comment on its implementation

1. All persons deprived of their liberty shall be treated with humanity and with respect for the inherent dignity of the human person.

2.

(a) Accused persons shall, save in exceptional circumstances, be segregated from convicted persons and shall be subject to separate treatment appropriate to their status as unconvicted persons;

(b) Accused juvenile persons shall be separated from adults and brought as speedily as possible for adjudication. 3. The penitentiary system shall comprise treatment of prisoners the essential aim of which shall be their reformation and social rehabilitation. Juvenile offenders shall be segregated from adults and be accorded treatment appropriate to their age and legal status.

Article 11

No one shall be imprisoned merely on the ground of inability to fulfil a contractual obligation.

Article 12 General comment on its implementation

1. Everyone lawfully within the territory of a State shall, within that territory, have the right to liberty of movement and freedom to choose his residence.

2. Everyone shall be free to leave any country, including his own.

3. The above-mentioned rights shall not be subject to any restrictions except those which are provided by law, are necessary to protect national security, public order (ordre public), public health or morals or the rights and freedoms of others, and are consistent with the other rights recognized in the present Covenant.

4. No one shall be arbitrarily deprived of the right to enter his own country.

Article 13

An alien lawfully in the territory of a State Party to the present Covenant may be expelled therefrom only in pursuance of a decision reached in accordance with law and shall, except where compelling reasons of national security otherwise require, be allowed to submit the reasons against his expulsion and to have his case reviewed by, and be represented for the purpose before, the competent authority or a person or persons especially designated by the competent authority.

Article 14 General comment on its implementation

1. All persons shall be equal before the courts and tribunals. In the determination of any criminal charge against him, or of his rights and obligations in a suit at law, everyone shall be entitled to a fair and public hearing by a competent, independent and impartial tribunal established by law. The press and the public may be excluded from all or part of a trial for reasons

of morals, public order (ordre public) or national security in a democratic society, or when the interest of the private lives of the parties so requires, or to the extent strictly necessary in the opinion of the court in special circumstances where publicity would prejudice the interests of justice; but any judgement rendered in a criminal case or in a suit at law shall be made public except where the interest of juvenile persons otherwise requires or the proceedings concern matrimonial disputes or the guardianship of children.

2. Everyone charged with a criminal offence shall have the right to be presumed innocent until proved guilty according to law.

3. In the determination of any criminal charge against him, everyone shall be entitled to the following minimum guarantees, in full equality:

   (a) To be informed promptly and in detail in a language which he understands of the nature and cause of the charge against him;

   (b) To have adequate time and facilities for the preparation of his defence and to communicate with counsel of his own choosing;

   (c) To be tried without undue delay;

   (d) To be tried in his presence, and to defend himself in person or through legal assistance of his own choosing; to be informed, if he does not have legal assistance, of this right; and to have legal assistance assigned to him, in any case where the interests of justice so require, and without payment by him in any such case if he does not have sufficient means to pay for it;

(e) To examine, or have examined, the witnesses against him and to obtain the attendance and examination of witnesses on his behalf under the same conditions as witnesses against him;

(f) To have the free assistance of an interpreter if he cannot understand or speak the language used in court;

(g) Not to be compelled to testify against himself or to confess guilt.

4. In the case of juvenile persons, the procedure shall be such as will take account of their age and the desirability of promoting their rehabilitation.

5. Everyone convicted of a crime shall have the right to his conviction and sentence being reviewed by a higher tribunal according to law.

6. When a person has by a final decision been convicted of a criminal offence and when subsequently his conviction has been reversed or he has been pardoned on the ground that a new or newly discovered fact shows conclusively that there has been a miscarriage of justice, the person who has suffered punishment as a result of such conviction shall be compensated according to law, unless it is proved that the non-disclosure of the unknown fact in time is wholly or partly attributable to him.

7. No one shall be liable to be tried or punished again for an offence for which he has already been finally convicted or acquitted in accordance with the law and penal procedure of each country.

Article 15

1. No one shall be held guilty of any criminal offence on account of any act or omission which did not constitute a criminal offence, under national or international law, at the time when it was committed. Nor shall a heavier penalty be imposed than the one that was applicable at the time when the criminal offence was committed. If, subsequent to the commission of the offence, provision is made by law for the imposition of the lighter penalty, the offender shall benefit thereby.
2. Nothing in this article shall prejudice the trial and punishment of any person for any act or omission which, at the time when it was committed, was criminal according to the general principles of law recognized by the community of nations.

Article 16

Everyone shall have the right to recognition everywhere as a person before the law.

Article 17 General comment on its implementation

1. No one shall be subjected to arbitrary or unlawful interference with his privacy, family, home or correspondence, nor to unlawful attacks on his honour and reputation.
2. Everyone has the right to the protection of the law against such interference or attacks.

Article 18 General comment on its implementation

1. Everyone shall have the right to freedom of thought, conscience and religion. This right shall include freedom to have or to adopt a religion or belief of his choice, and freedom, either individually or in community with others and in public or private, to manifest his religion or belief in worship, observance, practice and teaching.
2. No one shall be subject to coercion which would impair his freedom to have or to adopt a religion or belief of his choice.
3. Freedom to manifest one's religion or beliefs may be subject only to such limitations as are prescribed by law and are necessary to protect public safety, order, health, or morals or the fundamental rights and freedoms of others. 4. The States Parties to the present Covenant undertake to have respect for the liberty of parents and, when applicable, legal guardians to ensure the religious and moral education of their children in conformity with their own convictions.

Article 19 General comment on its implementation

1. Everyone shall have the right to hold opinions without interference.
2. Everyone shall have the right to freedom of expression; this right shall include freedom to seek, receive and impart information and ideas of all kinds, regardless of frontiers, either orally, in writing or in print, in the form of art, or through any other media of his choice.

3. The exercise of the rights provided for in paragraph 2 of this article carries with it special duties and responsibilities. It may therefore be subject to certain restrictions, but these shall only be such as are provided by law and are necessary:
   (a) For respect of the rights or reputations of others;
   (b) For the protection of national security or of public order (ordre public), or of public health or morals.

Article 20 General comment on its implementation

1. Any propaganda for war shall be prohibited by law.
2. Any advocacy of national, racial or religious hatred that constitutes incitement to discrimination, hostility or violence shall be prohibited by law.

Article 21

The right of peaceful assembly shall be recognized. No restrictions may be placed on the exercise of this right other than those imposed in conformity with the law and which are necessary in a democratic society in the interests of national security or public safety, public order (ordre public), the protection of public health or morals or the protection of the rights and freedoms of others.

Article 22

1. Everyone shall have the right to freedom of association with others, including the right to form and join trade unions for the protection of his interests.

2. No restrictions may be placed on the exercise of this right other than those which are prescribed by law and which are necessary in a democratic society in the interests of national security or public safety, public order (ordre public), the protection of public health or morals or the protection of the rights and freedoms of others. This article shall not prevent the imposition of lawful restrictions on members of the armed forces and of the police in their exercise of this right.
3. Nothing in this article shall authorize States Parties to the International Labour Organisation Convention of 1948 concerning Freedom of Association and Protection of the Right to Organize to take legislative measures which would prejudice, or to apply the law in such a manner as to prejudice, the guarantees provided for in that Convention.

Article 23 General comment on its implementation

1. The family is the natural and fundamental group unit of society and is entitled to protection by society and the State.
2. The right of men and women of marriageable age to marry and to found a family shall be recognized.
3. No marriage shall be entered into without the free and full consent of the intending spouses.
4. States Parties to the present Covenant shall take appropriate steps to ensure equality of rights and responsibilities of spouses as to marriage, during marriage and at its dissolution. In the case of dissolution, provision shall be made for the necessary protection of any children.

Article 24 General comment on its implementation

1. Every child shall have, without any discrimination as to race, colour, sex, language, religion, national or social origin, property or birth, the right to such measures of protection as are required by his status as a minor, on the part of his family, society and the State.
2. Every child shall be registered immediately after birth and shall have a name.
3. Every child has the right to acquire a nationality.

Article 25 General comment on its implementation

Every citizen shall have the right and the opportunity, without any of the distinctions mentioned in article 2 and without unreasonable restrictions:

(a) To take part in the conduct of public affairs, directly or through freely chosen representatives;

(b) To vote and to be elected at genuine periodic elections which shall be by universal and equal suffrage and shall be held by secret ballot, guaranteeing the free expression of the will of the electors;

(c) To have access, on general terms of equality, to public service in his country.

Article 26

All persons are equal before the law and are entitled without any discrimination to the equal protection of the law. In this respect, the law shall prohibit any discrimination and guarantee to all persons equal and effective protection against discrimination on any ground such as race, colour, sex, language, religion, political or other opinion, national or social origin, property, birth or other status.

Article 27 General comment on its implementation

In those States in which ethnic, religious or linguistic minorities exist, persons belonging to such minorities shall not be denied the right, in community with the other members of their group, to enjoy their own culture, to profess and practise their own religion, or to use their own language.

PART IV

Article 28

1. There shall be established a Human Rights Committee (hereafter referred to in the present Covenant as the Committee). It shall consist of eighteen members and shall carry out the functions hereinafter provided.
2. The Committee shall be composed of nationals of the States Parties to the present Covenant who shall be persons of high moral character and recognized competence in the field of human rights, consideration being given to the usefulness of the participation of some persons having legal experience.
3. The members of the Committee shall be elected and shall serve in their personal capacity.

Article 29

1. The members of the Committee shall be elected by secret ballot from a list of persons possessing the qualifications prescribed in article 28 and nominated for the purpose by the States Parties to the present Covenant.
2. Each State Party to the present Covenant may nominate not more than two persons. These persons shall be nationals of the nominating State.
3. A person shall be eligible for renomination.

Article 30

1. The initial election shall be held no later than six months after the date of the entry into force of the present Covenant.
2. At least four months before the date of each election to the Committee, other than an election to fill a vacancy declared in accordance with article 34, the Secretary-General of the United Nations shall address a written invitation to the States Parties to the present Covenant to submit their nominations for membership of the Committee within three months.
3. The Secretary-General of the United Nations shall prepare a list in alphabetical order of all the persons thus nominated, with an indication of the States Parties which have nominated them, and shall submit it to the States Parties to the present Covenant no later than one month before the date of each election.

4. Elections of the members of the Committee shall be held at a meeting of the States Parties to the present Covenant convened by the Secretary General of the United Nations at the Headquarters of the United Nations. At that meeting, for which two thirds of the States Parties to the present Covenant shall constitute a quorum, the persons elected to the Committee shall be those nominees who obtain the largest number of votes and an absolute majority of the votes of the representatives of States Parties present and voting.

Article 31

1. The Committee may not include more than one national of the same State.
2. In the election of the Committee, consideration shall be given to equitable geographical distribution of membership and to the representation of the different forms of civilization and of the principal legal systems.

Article 32

1. The members of the Committee shall be elected for a term of four years. They shall be eligible for re-election if renominated. However, the terms of nine of the members elected at the first election shall expire at the end of two years; immediately after the first election, the names of these nine members shall be chosen by lot by the Chairman of the meeting referred to in article 30, paragraph 4.
2. Elections at the expiry of office shall be held in accordance with the preceding articles of this part of the present Covenant.

Article 33

1. If, in the unanimous opinion of the other members, a member of the Committee has ceased to carry out his functions for any cause other than absence of a temporary character, the Chairman of the Committee shall notify the Secretary-General of the United Nations, who shall then declare the seat of that member to be vacant.
2. In the event of the death or the resignation of a member of the Committee, the Chairman shall immediately notify the Secretary-General of the United Nations, who shall declare the seat vacant from the date of death or the date on which the resignation takes effect.

Article 34

1. When a vacancy is declared in accordance with article 33 and if the term of office of the member to be replaced does not expire within six months of the declaration of the vacancy, the Secretary-General of the United Nations shall notify each of the States Parties to the present Covenant, which may within two months submit nominations in accordance with article 29 for the purpose of filling the vacancy.
2. The Secretary-General of the United Nations shall prepare a list in alphabetical order of the persons thus nominated and shall submit it to the States Parties to the present Covenant. The election to fill the vacancy shall then take place in accordance with the relevant provisions of this part of the present Covenant.

3. A member of the Committee elected to fill a vacancy declared in accordance with article 33 shall hold office for the remainder of the term of the member who vacated the seat on the Committee under the provisions of that article.

Article 35

The members of the Committee shall, with the approval of the General Assembly of the United Nations, receive emoluments from United Nations resources on such terms and conditions as the General Assembly may decide, having regard to the importance of the Committee's responsibilities.

Article 36

The Secretary-General of the United Nations shall provide the necessary staff and facilities for the effective performance of the functions of the Committee under the present Covenant.

Article 37

1. The Secretary-General of the United Nations shall convene the initial meeting of the Committee at the Headquarters of the United Nations.
2. After its initial meeting, the Committee shall meet at such times as shall be provided in its rules of procedure.
3. The Committee shall normally meet at the Headquarters of the United Nations or at the United Nations Office at Geneva.

Article 38

Every member of the Committee shall, before taking up his duties, make a solemn declaration in open committee that he will perform his functions impartially and conscientiously.

Article 39

1. The Committee shall elect its officers for a term of two years. They may be re-elected.
2. The Committee shall establish its own rules of procedure, but these rules shall provide, inter alia, that:
   (a) Twelve members shall constitute a quorum;
   (b) Decisions of the Committee shall be made by a majority vote of the members present.

Article 40

1. The States Parties to the present Covenant undertake to submit reports on the measures they have adopted which give effect to the rights recognized herein and on the progress made in the enjoyment of those rights:
   (a) Within one year of the entry into force of the present Covenant for the States Parties concerned;
   (b) Thereafter whenever the Committee so requests.
2. All reports shall be submitted to the Secretary-General of the United Nations, who shall transmit

them to the Committee for consideration. Reports shall indicate the factors and difficulties, if any, affecting the implementation of the present Covenant.

3. The Secretary-General of the United Nations may, after consultation with the Committee, transmit to the specialized agencies concerned copies of such parts of the reports as may fall within their field of competence.

4. The Committee shall study the reports submitted by the States Parties to the present Covenant. It shall transmit its reports, and such general comments as it may consider appropriate, to the States Parties. The Committee may also transmit to the Economic and Social Council these comments along with the copies of the reports it has received from States Parties to the present Covenant.

5. The States Parties to the present Covenant may submit to the Committee observations on any comments that may be made in accordance with paragraph 4 of this article.

Article 41 General comment on its implementation

1. A State Party to the present Covenant may at any time declare under this article that it recognizes the competence of the Committee to receive and consider communications to the effect that a State Party claims that another State Party is not fulfilling its obligations under the present Covenant. Communications under this article may be received and considered only if submitted by a State Party which has made a declaration recognizing in regard to itself the

competence of the Committee. No communication shall be received by the Committee if it concerns a State Party which has not made such a declaration. Communications received under this article shall be dealt with in accordance with the following procedure:

(a) If a State Party to the present Covenant considers that another State Party is not giving effect to the provisions of the present Covenant, it may, by written communication, bring the matter to the attention of that State Party. Within three months after the receipt of the communication the receiving State shall afford the State which sent the communication an explanation, or any other statement in writing clarifying the matter which should include, to the extent possible and pertinent, reference to domestic procedures and remedies taken, pending, or available in the matter;

(b) If the matter is not adjusted to the satisfaction of both States Parties concerned within six months after the receipt by the receiving State of the initial communication, either State shall have the right to refer the matter to the Committee, by notice given to the Committee and to the other State;

(c) The Committee shall deal with a matter referred to it only after it has ascertained that all available domestic remedies have been invoked and exhausted in the matter, in conformity with the generally recognized principles of international law. This shall not be the rule where the application of the remedies is unreasonably prolonged;

(d) The Committee shall hold closed meetings when examining communications under this article;

(e) Subject to the provisions of subparagraph ©, the Committee shall make available its good offices to the States Parties concerned with a view to a friendly solution of the matter on the basis of respect for human rights and fundamental freedoms as recognized in the present Covenant;

(f) In any matter referred to it, the Committee may call upon the States Parties concerned, referred to in subparagraph (b), to supply any relevant information;

(g) The States Parties concerned, referred to in subparagraph (b), shall have the right to be represented when the matter is being considered in the Committee and to make submissions orally and/or in writing;

(h) The Committee shall, within twelve months after the date of receipt of notice under subparagraph (b), submit a report:

(i) If a solution within the terms of subparagraph (e) is reached, the Committee shall confine its report to a brief statement of the facts and of the solution reached;

(ii) If a solution within the terms of subparagraph (e) is not reached, the Committee shall confine its report to a brief statement of the facts; the written submissions and record of the oral submissions made by the States Parties concerned shall be attached to the report. In every matter, the report shall be communicated to the States Parties concerned.

2. The provisions of this article shall come into force when ten States Parties to the present Covenant have made declarations under paragraph I of this article. Such declarations shall be deposited by the States Parties with the Secretary-General of the United Nations, who shall transmit copies thereof to the other States Parties. A declaration may be withdrawn at any time by notification to the Secretary-General. Such a withdrawal shall not prejudice the consideration of any matter which is the subject of a communication already transmitted under this article; no further communication by any State Party shall be received after the notification of withdrawal of the declaration has been received by the Secretary-General, unless the State Party concerned has made a new declaration.

Article 42

1.

(a) If a matter referred to the Committee in accordance with article 41 is not resolved to the satisfaction of the States Parties concerned, the Committee may, with the prior consent of the States Parties concerned, appoint an ad hoc Conciliation Commission (hereinafter referred to as the Commission). The good offices of the Commission shall be made available to the States Parties concerned with a view to an amicable solution of the matter on the basis of respect for the present Covenant;

(b) Thc Commission shall consist of five persons acceptable to the States Parties concerned. If the States Parties concerned fail to reach agreement within three months on all or part of the composition of the Commission, the members of the Commission concerning whom no agreement has been reached shall be elected by secret ballot by a two-thirds majority vote of the Committee from among its members.

2. The members of the Commission shall serve in their personal capacity. They shall not be nationals of the States Parties concerned, or of a State not Party to the present Covenant, or of a State Party which has not made a declaration under article 41.

3. The Commission shall elect its own Chairman and adopt its own rules of procedure.

4. The meetings of the Commission shall normally be held at the Headquarters of the United Nations or at the United Nations Office at Geneva. However, they may be held at such other convenient places as the Commission may determine in consultation with the Secretary-General of the United Nations and the States Parties concerned.

5. The secretariat provided in accordance with article 36 shall also service the commissions appointed under this article.

6. The information received and collated by the Committee shall be made available to the Commission and the Commission may call upon the States Parties concerned to supply any other relevant information. 7. When the Commission has fully considered the matter, but in any event not later than twelve months after having been seized of the matter, it shall submit to the Chairman of the Committee a report for communication to the States Parties concerned:

(a) If the Commission is unable to complete its consideration of the matter within twelve months, it shall confine its report to a brief statement of the status of its consideration of the matter;

(b) If an amicable solution to the matter on tie basis of respect for human rights as recognized in the present Covenant is reached, the Commission shall confine its report to a brief statement of the facts and of the solution reached;

(c) If a solution within the terms of subparagraph (b) is not reached, the Commission's report shall embody its findings on all questions of fact relevant to the issues between the States Parties concerned, and its views on the possibilities of an amicable solution of the matter. This report shall also contain the written submissions and a record of the oral submissions made by the States Parties concerned;

(d) If the Commission's report is submitted under subparagraph ©, the States Parties concerned shall, within three months of the receipt of the report, notify the Chairman of the Committee whether or not they accept the contents of the report of the Commission.

8. The provisions of this article are without prejudice to the responsibilities of the Committee under article 41.

9. The States Parties concerned shall share equally all the expenses of the members of the Commission in accordance with estimates to be provided by the Secretary-General of the United Nations.

10. The Secretary-General of the United Nations shall be empowered to pay the expenses of the members of the Commission, if necessary, before reimbursement by the States Parties concerned, in accordance with paragraph 9 of this article.

Article 43

The members of the Committee, and of the ad hoc conciliation commissions which may be appointed under article 42, shall be entitled to the facilities, privileges and immunities of experts on mission for the United Nations as laid down in the relevant sections of the Convention on the Privileges and Immunities of the United Nations.

Article 44

The provisions for the implementation of the present Covenant shall apply without prejudice to the procedures prescribed in the field of human rights by or under the constituent instruments and the conventions of the United Nations and of the specialized agencies and shall not prevent the States Parties to the present Covenant from having recourse to other procedures for settling a dispute in accordance with general or special international agreements in force between them.

Article 45

The Committee shall submit to the General Assembly of the United Nations, through the Economic and Social Council, an annual report on its activities.

PART V

Article 46

Nothing in the present Covenant shall be interpreted as impairing the provisions of the Charter of the United Nations and of the constitutions of the specialized agencies which define the respective responsibilities of the various organs of the United Nations and of the specialized agencies in regard to the matters dealt with in the present Covenant.

Article 47

Nothing in the present Covenant shall be interpreted as impairing the inherent right of all peoples to enjoy and utilize fully and freely their natural wealth and resources.

PART VI

Article 48

1. The present Covenant is open for signature by any State Member of the United Nations or member of any of its specialized agencies, by any State Party to the Statute of the International Court of Justice, and by any other State which has been invited by the General Assembly of the United Nations to become a Party to the present Covenant.
2. The present Covenant is subject to ratification. Instruments of ratification shall be deposited with the Secretary-General of the United Nations.
3. The present Covenant shall be open to accession by any State referred to in paragraph 1 of this article.

4. Accession shall be effected by the deposit of an instrument of accession with the Secretary-General of the United Nations.

5. The Secretary-General of the United Nations shall inform all States which have signed this Covenant or acceded to it of the deposit of each instrument of ratification or accession.

Article 49

1. The present Covenant shall enter into force three months after the date of the deposit with the Secretary-General of the United Nations of the thirty-fifth instrument of ratification or instrument of accession.

2. For each State ratifying the present Covenant or acceding to it after the deposit of the thirty-fifth instrument of ratification or instrument of accession, the present Covenant shall enter into force three months after the date of the deposit of its own instrument of ratification or instrument of accession.

Article 50

The provisions of the present Covenant shall extend to all parts of federal States without any limitations or exceptions.

Article 51

1. Any State Party to the present Covenant may propose an amendment and file it with the Secretary-

General of the United Nations. The Secretary-General of the United Nations shall thereupon communicate any proposed amendments to the States Parties to the present Covenant with a request that they notify him whether they favour a conference of States Parties for the purpose of considering and voting upon the proposals. In the event that at least one third of the States Parties favours such a conference, the Secretary-General shall convene the conference under the auspices of the United Nations. Any amendment adopted by a majority of the States Parties present and voting at the conference shall be submitted to the General Assembly of the United Nations for approval.

2. Amendments shall come into force when they have been approved by the General Assembly of the United Nations and accepted by a two-thirds majority of the States Parties to the present Covenant in accordance with their respective constitutional processes.

3. When amendments come into force, they shall be binding on those States Parties which have accepted them, other States Parties still being bound by the provisions of the present Covenant and any earlier amendment which they have accepted.

Article 52

Irrespective of the notifications made under article 48, paragraph 5, the Secretary-General of the United Nations shall inform all States referred to in paragraph I of the same article of the following particulars:

(a) Signatures, ratifications and accessions under article 48;

(b) The date of the entry into force of the present Covenant under article 49 and the date of the entry into force of any amendments under article 51.

Article 53

1. The present Covenant, of which the Chinese, English, French, Russian and Spanish texts are equally authentic, shall be deposited in the archives of the United Nations.

2. The Secretary-General of the United Nations shall transmit certified copies of the present Covenant to all States referred to in article 48.

6

International Convention on the Elimination of All Forms of Racial Discrimination

(New York 7 March 1966)

The States Parties to this Convention,

Considering that the Charter of the United Nations is based on the principles of the dignity and equality inherent in all human beings, and that all Member States have pledged themselves to take joint and separate action, in cooperation with the Organization, for the achievement of one of the purposes of the United Nations which is to promote and encourage universal respect for and observance of human rights and fundamental freedoms for all, without distinction as to race, sex, language or religion,

Considering that the Universal Declaration of Human Rights proclaims that all human beings are born free and equal in dignity and rights and that everyone is entitled to all the rights and freedoms set out therein, without distinction of any kind, in particular as to race, colour or national origin,

Considering that all human beings are equal before the law and are entitled to equal protection of the law against any discrimination and against any incitement to discrimination,

Considering that the United Nations has condemned colonialism and all practices of segregation and discrimination associated therewith, in whatever form and wherever they exist, and that the Declaration on the Granting of Independence to Colonial Countries and Peoples of 14 December 1960 (General Assembly resolution 1514 (XV)) has affirmed and solemnly proclaimed the necessity of bringing them to a speedy and unconditional end,

Considering that the United Nations Declaration on the Elimination of All Forms of Racial Discrimination of 20 November 1963 (General Assembly resolution 1904 (XVIII)) solemnly affirms the necessity of speedily eliminating racial discrimination throughout the world in all its forms and manifestations and of securing understanding of and respect for the dignity of the human person,

Convinced that any doctrine of superiority based on racial differentiation is scientifically false, morally condemnable, socially unjust and dangerous, and that there is no justification for racial discrimination, in theory or in practice, anywhere,

Reaffirming that discrimination between human beings on the grounds of race, colour or ethnic origin in an obstacle to friendly and peaceful relations among nations and is capable of disturbing peace and security among peoples and the harmony of persons living side by side even within one and the same State,

Convinced that the existence of racial barriers is repugnant to the ideals of any human society,

Alarmed by manifestations of racial discrimination still in evidence in some areas of the world and by governmental policies based on racial superiority or hatred, such as policies of apartheid, segregation or separation,

Resolved to adopt all necessary measures for speedily eliminating racial discrimination in all its forms and manifestations, and to prevent and combat racist doctrines and practices in order to promote understanding between races and to build an international community free from all forms of racial segregation and racial discrimination,

Bearing in mind the Convention concerning Discrimination in respect of Employment and Occupation adopted by the International Labour Organisation in 1958, and the Convention against Discrimination in Education adopted by the United Nations Educational, Scientific and Cultural Organization in 1960,

Desiring to implement the principles embodied in the United Nations Declaration on the Elimination of All Forms of Racial Discrimination and to secure the earliest adoption of practical measures to that end,

Have agreed as follows:

PART I

Article 1

In this Convention, the term "racial discrimination" shall mean any distinction, exclusion, restriction or preference based on race, colour, descent, or national or ethnic origin which has the purpose or effect of nullifying or impairing the recognition, enjoyment or exercise, on an equal footing, of human rights and fundamental freedoms in the political, economic, social, cultural or any other field of public life.

This Convention shall not apply to distinctions, exclusions, restrictions or preferences made by a State Party to this Convention between citizens and non-citizens.

Nothing in this Convention may be interpreted as affecting in any way the legal provisions of States Parties concerning nationality, citizenship or naturalization, provided that such provisions do not discriminate against any particular nationality.

Special measures taken for the sole purpose of securing adequate advancement of certain racial or ethnic groups or individuals requiring such protection as may be necessary in order to ensure such groups or individuals equal enjoyment or exercise of human rights and fundamental freedoms shall not be deemed racial discrimination, provided, however, that such measures do not, as a consequence, lead to the maintenance of separate rights for different racial groups and that they shall not be continued after the objectives for which they were taken have been achieved.

Article 2

States Parties condemn racial discrimination and undertake to pursue by all appropriate means and without delay a policy of eliminating racial discrimination in all its forms and promoting understanding among all races, and, to this end:

(a) Each State Party undertakes to engage in no act or practice of racial discrimination against persons, groups of persons or institutions and to ensure that all public authorities and public institutions, national and local, shall act in conformity with this obligation;

(b) Each State Party undertakes not to sponsor, defend or support racial discrimination by any persons or organizations;

(c) Each State Party shall take effective measures to review governmental, national and local policies, and to amend, rescind or nullify any laws and regulations which have the effect of creating or perpetuating racial discrimination wherever it exists;

(d) Each State Party shall prohibit and bring to an end, by all appropriate means, including legislation as required by circumstances, racial discrimination by any persons, group or organization;

(e) Each State Party undertakes to encourage, where appropriate, integrationist multi-racial organizations and movements and other means of eliminating barriers between races, and to discourage anything which tends to strengthen racial division.

States Parties shall, when the circumstances so warrant, take, in the social, economic, cultural and other fields, special and concrete measures to ensure the adequate development and protection of certain racial groups or individuals belonging to them, for the purpose of guaranteeing them the full and equal enjoyment of human rights and fundamental freedoms. These measures shall in no case entail as a consequence the maintenance of unequal or separate rights for different racial groups after the objectives for which they were taken have been achieved.

Article 3

States Parties particularly condemn racial segregation and apartheid and undertake to prevent, prohibit and eradicate all practices of this nature in territories under their jurisdiction.

Article 4

States Parties condemn all propaganda and all organizations which are based on ideas or theories of superiority of one race or group of persons of one colour or ethnic origin, or which attempt to justify or promote racial hatred and discrimination in any form, and undertake to adopt immediate and positive measures designed to eradicate all incitement to, or acts of, such discrimination and, to this end, with due regard to the principles embodied in the Universal Declaration of Human Rights and the rights expressly set forth in article 5 of this Convention, inter alia:

(a) Shall declare an offence punishable by law all dissemination of ideas based on racial superiority or hatred, incitement to racial discrimination, as well as all acts of violence or incitement to such acts against any race or group of persons of another colour or ethnic origin, and also the provision of any assistance to racist activities, including the financing thereof;

(b) Shall declare illegal and prohibit organizations, and also organized and all other propaganda activities, which promote and incite racial discrimination, and shall recognize participation in such organizations or activities as an offence punishable by law;

(c) Shall not permit public authorities or public institutions, national or local, to promote or incite racial discrimination.

Article 5

In compliance with the fundamental obligations laid down in article 2 of this Convention, States Parties undertake to prohibit and to eliminate racial discrimination in all its forms and to guarantee the right of everyone, without distinction as to race, colour, or national or ethnic origin, to equality before the law, notably in the enjoyment of the following rights:

(a) The right to equal treatment before the tribunals and all other organs administering justice;

(b) The right to security of person and protection by the State against violence or bodily harm, whether inflicted by government officials or by any individual, group or institution;

(c) Political rights, in particular the rights to participate in elections—to vote and to stand for election—on the basis of universal and equal suffrage, to take part in the Government as well as in the conduct of public affairs at any level and to have equal access to public service;

(d) Other civil rights, in particular:

(i) The right to freedom of movement and residence within the border of the State;

(ii) The right to leave any country, including one's own, and to return to one's country;

(iii) The right to nationality;

(iv) The right to marriage and choice of spouse;

(v) The right to own property alone as well as in association with others;

(vi) The right to inherit;

(vii) The right to freedom of thought, conscience and religion;

(viii) The right to freedom of opinion and expression;

(ix) The right to freedom of peaceful assembly and association;

(e) Economic, social and cultural rights, in particular:

(i) The rights to work, to free choice of employment, to just and favourable conditions of work, to protection against unemployment, to equal pay for equal work, to just and favourable remuneration;

(ii) The right to form and join trade unions;

(iii) The right to housing;

(iv) The right to public health, medical care, social security and social services;

(v) The right to education and training;

(vi) The right to equal participation in cultural activities;

(f) The right of access to any place or service intended for use by the general public, such as transport, hotels, restaurants, cafes, theatres and parks.

Article 6

States Parties shall assure to everyone within their jurisdiction effective protection and remedies, through the competent national tribunals and other State institutions, against any acts of racial discrimination which violate his human rights and fundamental freedoms contrary to this Convention, as well as the right to seek from such tribunals just and adequate reparation or satisfaction for any damage suffered as a result of such discrimination.

Article 7

States Parties undertake to adopt immediate and effective measures, particularly in the fields of teaching, education, culture and information, with a view to combating prejudices which lead to racial discrimination and to promoting understanding, tolerance and friendship among nations and racial or ethnical groups, as well as to propagating the purposes and principles of the Charter of the United Nations, the Universal Declaration of Human Rights, the United Nations Declaration on the Elimination of All Forms of Racial Discrimination, and this Convention.

PART II

Article 8

There shall be established a Committee on the Elimination of Racial Discrimination (hereinafter referred to as the Committee) consisting of eighteen experts of high moral standing and acknowledged impartiality elected by States Parties from among their nationals, who shall serve in their personal capacity, consideration being given to equitable geographical distribution and to the representation of the different forms of civilization as well as of the principal legal systems.

The members of the Committee shall be elected by secret ballot from a list of persons nominated by the States Parties. Each State Party may nominate one person from among its own nationals.

The initial election shall be held six months after the date of the entry into force of this Convention. At least three months before the date of each election the Secretary-General of the United Nations shall address a letter to the States Parties inviting them to submit their nominations within two months. The Secretary-General shall prepare a list in alphabetical order of all persons thus nominated, indicating the States Parties which have nominated them, and shall submit it to the States Parties.

Elections of the members of the Committee shall be held at a meeting of States Parties convened by the Secretary-General at United Nations Headquarters. At that meeting, for which two-thirds of the States Parties shall constitute a quorum, the persons elected to the Committee shall be those nominees who obtain the largest number of votes and an absolute majority of the votes of the representatives of States Parties present and voting.

(a) The members of the Committee shall be elected for a term of four years. However, the terms of nine of the members elected at the first election shall expire at the end of two years; immediately after the first election the names of these nine members shall be chosen by lot by the Chairman of the Committee.

(b) For the filling of casual vacancies, the State Party whose expert has ceased to function as a member of the Committee shall appoint another expert from among its nationals, subject to the approval of the Committee.

States Parties shall be responsible for the expenses of the members of the Committee while they are in performance of Committee duties.

Article 9

States Parties undertake to submit to the Secretary-General of the United Nations, for consideration by the Committee, a report on the legislative, judicial, administrative or other measures which they have adopted and which give effect to the provisions of this Convention: (a) within one year after the entry into force of the Convention for the State concerned; and (b) thereafter every two years and whenever the Committee so requests. The Committee may request further information from the States Parties.

The Committee shall report annually, through the Secretary-General, to the General Assembly of the United Nations on its activities and may make suggestions and general recommendations based on the examination of the reports and information received from the States Parties. Such suggestions and general recommendations shall be reported to the General Assembly together with comments, if any, from States Parties.

Article 10

— The Committee shall adopt its own rules of procedure.

— The Committee shall elect its officers for a term of two years.

— The secretariat of the Committee shall be provided by the Secretary-General of the United Nations.

— The meetings of the Committee shall normally be held at United Nations Headquarters.

Article 11

If a State Party considers that another State Party is not giving effect to the provisions of this Convention, it may bring the matter to the attention of the Committee. The Committee shall then transmit the communication to the State Party concerned. Within three months, the receiving State shall submit to the Committee written explanations or statements clarifying the matter and the remedy, if any, that may have been taken by that State.

If the matter is not adjusted to the satisfaction of both parties, either by bilateral negotiations or by any other procedure open to them, within six months after the receipt by the receiving State of the initial communication, either State shall have the right to refer the matter again to the Committee by notifying the Committee and also the other State.

The Committee shall deal with a matter referred to it in accordance with paragraph 2 of this article after it has ascertained that all available domestic remedies have been invoked and exhausted in the case, in conformity with the generally recognized principles of international law. This shall not be the rule where the application of the remedies is unreasonably prolonged.

In any matter referred to it, the Committee may call upon the States Parties concerned to supply any other relevant information.

When any matter arising out of this article is being considered by the Committee, the States Parties concerned shall be entitled to send a representative to take part in the proceedings of the Committee, without voting rights, while the matter is under consideration.

Article 12

(a) After the Committee has obtained and collated all the information it deems necessary, the Chairman shall appoint an ad hoc Conciliation Commission (hereinafter referred to as the Commission) comprising five persons who may or may not be members of the Committee. The members of the Commission shall be appointed with the unanimous consent of the parties to the dispute, and its good offices shall be made available to the States concerned with a view to an amicable solution of the matter on the basis of respect for this Convention.

(b) If the States parties to the dispute fail to reach agreement within three months on all or part of the composition of the Commission, the members of the Commission not agreed upon by the States parties to the dispute shall be elected by secret ballot by a two-thirds majority vote of the Committee from among its own members.

— The members of the Commission shall serve in their personal capacity. They shall not be nationals of the States parties to the dispute or of a State not Party to this Convention.

— The Commission shall elect its own Chairman and adopt its own rules of procedure.

— The meetings of the Commission shall normally be held at United Nations Headquarters or at any other convenient place as determined by the Commission.

— The secretariat provided in accordance with article 10, paragraph 3, of this Convention shall also service the Commission whenever a dispute among States Parties brings the Commission into being.

— The States parties to the dispute shall share equally all the expenses of the members of the Commission in accordance with estimates to be provided by the Secretary-General of the United Nations.

— The Secretary-General shall be empowered to pay the expenses of the members of the Commission, if necessary, before reimbursement by the States parties to the dispute in accordance with paragraph 6 of this article.

— The information obtained and collated by the Committee shall be made available to the Commission, and the Commission may call upon the States concerned to supply any other relevant information.

Article 13

When the Commission has fully considered the matter, it shall prepare and submit to the Chairman of the Committee a report embodying its findings on all questions of fact relevant to the issue between the parties and containing such recommendations as it may think proper for the amicable solution of the dispute.

The Chairman of the Committee shall communicate the report of the Commission to each of the States parties to the dispute. These States shall, within three months, inform the Chairman of the Committee whether or not they accept the recommendations contained in the report of the Commission.

After the period provided for in paragraph 2 of this article, the Chairman of the Committee shall communicate the report of the Commission and the declarations of the States Parties concerned to the other States Parties to this Convention.

Article 14

A State Party may at any time declare that it recognizes the competence of the Committee to receive and consider communications from individuals or groups of individuals within its jurisdiction claiming to be victims of a violation by that State Party of any of the rights set forth in this Convention. No communication shall be received by the Committee if it concerns a State Party which has not made such a declaration.

Any State Party which makes a declaration as provided for in paragraph 1 of this article may establish or indicate a body within its national legal order which shall be competent to receive and consider petitions from individuals and groups of individuals within its jurisdiction who claim to be victims of a violation of any of the rights set forth in this Convention and who have exhausted other available local remedies.

A declaration made in accordance with paragraph 1 of this article and the name of any body established or indicated in accordance with paragraph 2 of this article shall be deposited by the State Party concerned with the Secretary-General of the United Nations, who shall transmit copies thereof to the other States Parties. A declaration may be withdrawn at any time by notification to the Secretary-General, but such a withdrawal shall not affect communications pending before the Committee.

A register of petitions shall be kept by the body established or indicated in accordance with paragraph 2 of this article, and certified copies of the register shall be filed annually through appropriate channels with the Secretary-General on the understanding that the contents shall not be publicly disclosed.

In the event of failure to obtain satisfaction from the body established or indicated in accordance with paragraph 2 of this article, the petitioner shall have the right to communicate the matter to the Committee within six months.

(a) The Committee shall confidentially bring any communication referred to it to the attention of the State Party alleged to be violating any provision of this Convention, but the identity of the individual or groups of individuals concerned shall not be revealed without his or their express consent. The Committee shall not receive anonymous communications.

(b) Within three months, the receiving State shall submit to the Committee written explanations or statements clarifying the matter and the remedy, if any, that may have been taken by that State.

   (a) The Committee shall consider communications in the light of all information made available to it by the State Party concerned and by the petitioner. The Committee shall not consider any communication from a petitioner unless it has ascertained that the petitioner has exhausted all available domestic remedies. However, this shall not be the rule where the application of the remedies is unreasonably prolonged.

   (b) The Committee shall forward its suggestions and recommendations, if any, to the State Party concerned and to the petitioner.

The Committee shall include in its annual report a summary of such communications and, where appropriate, a summary of the explanations and statements of the States Parties concerned and of its own suggestions and recommendations.

The Committee shall be competent to exercise the functions provided for in this article only when at least ten States Parties to this Convention are bound by declarations in accordance with paragraph 1 of this article.

Article 15

Pending the achievement of the objectives of the Declaration on the Granting of Independence to Colonial Countries and Peoples, contained in General Assembly resolution 1514 (XV) of 14 December 1960, the provisions of this Convention shall in no way limit the right of petition granted to these peoples by other international instruments or by the United Nations and its specialized agencies.

(a) The Committee established under article 8, paragraph 1, of this Convention shall receive copies of the petitions from, and submit expressions of opinion and recommendations on these petitions to, the bodies of the United Nations which deal with matters directly related to the principles and objectives of this Convention in their consideration of petitions from the inhabitants of Trust and Non-Self-Governing Territories and all other territories to which General Assembly resolution 1514 (XV) applies, relating to matters covered by this Convention which are before these bodies.

(b) The Committee shall receive from the competent bodies of the United Nations copies of the reports concerning the legislative, judicial, administrative or other measures directly related to the principles and objectives of this Convention applied by the administering Powers within the Territories mentioned in sub-paragraph (a) of this paragraph, and shall express opinions and make recommendations to these bodies.

The Committee shall include in its report to the General Assembly a summary of the petitions and reports it has received from United Nations bodies, and the expressions of opinion and recommendations of the Committee relating to the said petitions and reports.

The Committee shall request from the Secretary-General of the United Nations all information relevant to the objectives of this Convention and available to him regarding the Territories mentioned in paragraph 2 (a) of this article.

Article 16

The provisions of this Convention concerning the settlement of disputes or complaints shall be applied without prejudice to other procedures for settling disputes or complaints in the field of discrimination laid down in the constituent instruments of, or in conventions adopted by, the United Nations and its specialized agencies, and shall not prevent the States Parties from having recourse to other procedures for settling a dispute in accordance with general or special international agreements in force between them.

PART III

Article 17

This Convention is open for signature by any State Member of the United Nations or member of any of its specialized agencies, by any State Party to the Statute of the International Court of Justice, and by any other State which has been invited by the General Assembly of the United Nations to become a Party to this Convention.

This Convention is subject to ratification. Instruments of ratification shall be deposited with the Secretary-General of the United Nations.

Article 18

This Convention shall be open to accession by any State referred to in article 17, paragraph 1, of the Convention.

Accession shall be effected by the deposit of an instrument of accession with the Secretary-General of the United Nations.

Article 19

This Convention shall enter into force on the thirtieth day after the date of the deposit with the Secretary-General of the United Nations of the twenty-seventh instrument of ratification or instrument of accession.

For each State ratifying this Convention or acceding to it after the deposit of the twenty-seventh instrument of ratification or instrument of accession, the Convention shall enter into force on the thirtieth day after the date of the deposit of its own instrument of ratification or instrument of accession.

Article 20

The Secretary-General of the United Nations shall receive and circulate to all States which are or may become Parties to this Convention reservations made by States at the time of ratification or accession. Any State which objects to the reservation shall, within a period of ninety days from the date of the said communication, notify the Secretary-General that it does not accept it.

A reservation incompatible with the object and purpose of this Convention shall not be permitted, nor shall a reservation the effect of which would inhibit the operation of any of the bodies established by this

Convention be allowed. A reservation shall be considered incompatible or inhibitive if at least two-thirds of the States Parties to this Convention object to it.

Reservations may be withdrawn at any time by notification to this effect addressed to the Secretary-General. Such notification shall take effect on the date on which it is received.

Article 21

A State Party may denounce this Convention by written notification to the Secretary-General of the United Nations. Denunciation shall take effect one year after the date of receipt of the notification by the Secretary-General.

Article 22

Any dispute between two or more States Parties with respect to the interpretation or application of this Convention, which is not settled by negociation or by the procedures expressly provided for in this Convention, shall, at the request of any of the parties to the dispute, be referred to the International Court of Justice for decision, unless the disputants agree to another mode of settlement.

Article 23

A request for the revision of this Convention may be made at any time by any State Party by means of a notification in writing addressed to the Secretary-General of the United Nations.

The General Assembly of the United Nations shall decide upon the steps, if any, to be taken in respect of such a request.

Article 24

The Secretary-General of the United Nations shall inform all States referred to in article 17, paragraph 1, of this Convention of the following particulars

(a) Signatures, ratifications and accessions under articles 17 and 18;

(b) The date of entry into force of this Convention under article 19;

(c) Communications and declarations received under articles 14, 20 and 23;

(d) Denunciations under article 21.

Article 25

This Convention, of which the Chinese, English, French, Russian and Spanish texts are equally authentic, shall be deposited in the archives of the United Nations.

The Secretary-General of the United Nations shall transmit certified copies of this Convention to all States belonging to any of the categories mentioned in article 17, paragraph 1, of the Convention.

IN FAITH WHEREOF the undersigned, being duly authorized thereto by their respective Governments, have signed the present Convention, opened for signature at New York, on the seventh day of March, one thousand nine hundred and sixty-six.

7

United Nations' Convention on the Elimination of all Forms of Discrimination against Women

The states parties to the present Convention,

Noting that the Charter of the United Nations reaffirms faith in fundamental human rights, in the dignity and worth of the human person and in the equal rights of men and women,

Noting that the Universal Declaration of Human Rights affirms the principle of the inadmissibility of discrimination and proclaims that all human beings are born free and equal in dignity and rights and that everyone is entitled to all the rights and freedoms set forth therein, without distinction of any kind including distinction based on sex,

Noting that the States Parties to the International Covenants of Human Rights have the obligation to ensure the equal rights of men and women to enjoy all economic, social cultural, civil and political rights,

Considering the international conventions concluded under the auspices of the United Nations and the specialized agencies promoting equality of rights of men and women,

Noting also the resolutions, declarations and recommendations adopted by the United Nations and the specialized agencies promoting equality of rights of men and women,

Concerned, however, that despite these various instruments extensive discrimination against women continues to exist,

Recalling that discrimination against women violates the principles of equality of rights and respect for human dignity, is an obstacle to the participation of women, on equal terms with men, in the political, social, economic and cultural life of their countries, hampers the growth of the prosperity of society and the family and makes more difficult the full development of the potentialities of women in the service of their countries and of humanity,

Concerned that in situations of poverty women have the least access to food, health, education, training and opportunities for employment and other needs,

Convinced that the establishment of the new international economic order based on equity and justice will contribute significantly towards the promotion of equality between men and women,

Emphasizing that the eradication of apartheid, all forms of racism, racial discrimination, colonialism, neo-colonialism, aggression, foreign occupation and domination and interference in the internal affairs of States is essential to the full enjoyment of the rights of men and women,

Affirming that the strengthening of international peace and security, the relaxation of international tension, mutual cooperation among all States irrespective of their social and economic systems, general and complete disarmament, in particular nuclear disarmament under strict and effective international control the affirmation of the principles of justice, equality and mutual benefit in relations among countries and the realization of the right of peoples under alien and colonial domination and foreign occupation to self-determination and independence, as well as respect for national sovereignty and territorial integrity, will promote social progress and development and as a consequence will contribute to the attainment of full equality between men and women,

Convinced that the full and complete development of a country, the welfare of the world and the cause of peace require the maximum participation of women of equal terms with men in all fields,

Bearing in mind the great contribution of women to the welfare of the family and to the development of society, so far not fully recognized, the social significance of maternity and the role of both parents in the family and in the upbringing of children, and aware that the role of women in procreation should not be a basis for discrimination but that the upbringing of children requires a sharing of responsibility between men and women and society as a whole,

Aware that a change in the traditional role of men as well as the role of women in society and in the family is needed to achieve full equality between men and women,

Determined to implement the principles set forth in the Declaration on the Elimination of Discrimination against Women and, for that purpose, to adopt the measures required for the elimination of such discrimination in all its forms and manifestations,

Have agreed on the following :

Part I

Article I

For the purposes of the present Convention, the term "discrimination against women" shall mean any distinction, exclusion or restriction made on the basis of sex which has the effect or purpose of impairing or nullifying the recognition, enjoyment or exercise by women, irrespective of their marital status, on a basis of equality of men and women, of human rights and fundamental freedoms in the political, economic, social, cultural, civil or any other field.

Article 2

States Parties condemn discrimination against women in all its forms, agree to pursue by all appropriate means and without delay a policy of eliminating discrimination against women and, to this end, undertake:

(a) To embody the principle of the equality of men and women in their national constitutions or other appropriate legislation if not yet incorporated therein and to ensure, through law and other appropriate means, the practical realization of this principle;

(b) To adopt appropriate legislative and other measures, including sanctions where appropriate, prohibiting all discrimination against women;

(c) To establish legal protection of the rights of women on an equal basis with men and to ensure through competent national tribunals and other public institutions the effective protection of women against any act of discrimination;

(d) To refrain from engaging in any act or practice of discrimination against women and to ensure that public authorities and institutions shall act in conformity with this obligation;

(e) To take all appropriate measures to eliminate discrimination against women by any person, organization or enterprise;

(f) To take all appropriate measures, including legislation, to modify or abolish existing laws, regulations, customs and practices which constitute discrimination against women;

(g) To repeal all national penal provisions which constitute discrimination against women.

Article 3

States Parties shall take in all fields, in particular in the political, social, economic and cultural fields, all appropriate measures, including legislation, to ensure the full development and advancement of women, for the purpose of guaranteeing them the exercise and enjoyment of human rights and fundamental freedoms on a basis of equality with men.

Article 4

1. Adoption by States Parties of temporary special measures aimed at accelerating de facts equality

between men and women shall not be considered discrimination as defined in the present Convention, but shall in no way entail as a consequence the maintenance of unequal or separate standards; these measures shall be discontinued when the objectives of equality of opportunity and treatment have been achieved.

2. Adoption by States Parties of special measures, including those measures contained in the present Convention, aimed at protecting maternity shall not be considered discriminatory.

Article 5

States Parties shall take all appropriate measures:

(a) To modify the social and cultural patterns of conduct of men and women, with a view to achieving the elimination of prejudices and customary and all other practices which are based on the idea of the inferiority or the superiority of either of the sexes or on stereotyped roles for men and women;

(b) To ensure that family education includes a proper understanding of maternity as a social function and the recognition of the common responsibility of men and women in the upbringing and development of their children, it being understood that the interest of the children is the primordial consideration in all cases.

Article 6

States Parties shall take all appropriate measures, including legislation, to suppress all forms of traffic in women and exploitation of prostitution of women.

Part II

Article 7

States Parties shall take all appropriate measures to eliminate discrimination against women in the political and public life of the country and, in particular, shall ensure to women, on equal terms with men, the right:

(a) To vote in all elections and public referenda and to be eligible for election to all publicly elected bodies;

(b) To participate in the formulation of government policy and the implementation thereof and to hold public office and perform all public functions at all levels of government;

(c) To participate in non-governmental organizations and associations concerned with the public and political life of the country.

Article 8

States Parties shall take all appropriate measures to ensure to women, on equal terms with men and without any discrimination, the opportunity to represent their Governments at the international level and to participate in the work of international organizations.

Article 9

1. States Parties shall grant women equal rights with men to acquire, change or retain their nationality. They shall ensure in particular that neither marriage to an alien nor change of nationality by the husband

during marriage shall automatically change the nationality of the wife, render her stateless or force upon her the nationality of the husband.

2. States Parties shall grant women equal rights with men with respect to the nationality of their children.

Part III

Article 10

States Parties shall take all appropriate measures to eliminate discrimination against women in order to ensure to them equal rights with men in the field of education and in particular to ensure, on a basis of equality of men and women :

(a) The same conditions for career and vocational guidance, for access to studies and for the achievement of diplomas in educational establishments of all categories in rural as well as in urban areas; this equality shall be ensured in pre-school, general, technical, professional and higher technical education, as well as in all types of vocational training;

(b) Access to the same curricula, the same examinations, teaching staff with qualifications of the same standard and school premises and equipment of the same quality;

(c) The elimination of any stereotyped concept of the roles of men and women at all levels and in all forms of education by encouraging coeducation and other types of education which will help to achieve this aim and, in particular, by the revision of textbooks and school programmes and the adaptation of teaching methods;

(d) The same opportunities to benefit from scholarships and other study grants;

(e) The same opportunities for access to programmes of continuing education, including adult and functional literacy programmes, particularly those aimed at reducing, at the earliest possible time, any gap in education existing between men and women;

(f) The reduction of female student drop-out rates and the organization of programmes for girls and women who have left school prematurely;

(g) The same opportunities to participate actively in sports and physical education;

(h) Access to specific educational information to help to ensure the health and well-being of families, including information and advice on family planning.

Article 11

1. States Parties shall take all appropriate measures to eliminate discrimination against women in the field of employment in order to ensure, on a basis of equality of men and women, the same rights, in particular;

   (a) The right to work at an right of all human beings.

   (b) The right to the same employment opportunities, including the application of the same criteria for selection in matters of employment;

   (c) The right to free choice of profession and employment, the right to promotion, job security and all benefits and conditions of service and the right to receive vocational training and retraining, including apprenticeships, advanced vocational training and recurrent training;

(d) The right to equal remuneration, including benefits, and to equal treatment in respect of work of equal value, as well as equality of treatment in the evaluation of the quality of work;

(e) The right to social security, particularly in cases of retirement, unemployment, sickness, invalidity and old age and other incapacity to work, as well as right to paid leave;

(f) The right to protection of health and to safety in working conditions, including the safeguarding of the function of reproduction.

2. In order to prevent discrimination against women on the grounds of marriage or maternity and to ensure their effective right to work, States Parties shall take appropriate measures:

(a) To prohibit, subject to the imposition of sanctions, dismissal on the grounds of pregnancy or of maternity leave and discrimination in dismissals on the basis of marital status;

(b) To introduce maternity leave with pay or with comparable social benefits without loss of former employment, seniority or social allowances;

(c) To encourage the provision of the necessary supporting social services to enable parents to combine family obligations with work responsibilities and participation in public life, in particular through promoting the establishment and development of a network of child-care facilities;

(d) To provide special protection to women during pregnancy in types of work proved to be harmful to them.

3. Protective legislation relating to matters covered in this article shall be reviewed periodically in the light of scientific and technological knowledge and shall be revised, repealed or extended as necessary.

Article 12

1. States Parties shall take all appropriate measures to eliminate discrimination against women in the field of health care in order to ensure, on a basis of equality of men and women, access to health care services, including those related to family planning.

2. Notwithstanding the provisions of paragraph 1 of this article, States Parties shall ensure to women appropriate services in connection with pregnancy, confinement and the post-natal period, granting free services where necessary, as well as adequate nutrition during pregnancy and lactation.

Article 13

States Parties shall take all appropriate measures to eliminate discrimination against women in other areas of economic and social life in order to ensure, on a basis of equality of men and women, the same rights, in particular:

(a) The right to family benefits;

(b) The right to bank loans, mortgages and other forms of financial credit;

(c) The right to participate in recreational activities, sports and all aspects of cultural life.

Article 14

1. States Parties shall take into account the particular problems faced by rural women and the significant roles which rural women play in the economic survival of their families, including their work in the nonmonetized sectors of the economy, and shall take all appropriate measures to ensure the application of the provisions of the present Convention to women in rural areas.

2. States Parties shall take all appropriate measures to eliminate discrimination against women in rural areas in order to ensure, on a basis of equality of men and women, that they participate in and benefit from rural development and, in particular, shall ensure to such women the right:

   (a) To participate in the elaboration and implementation of development planning at all levels;

   (b) To have access to adequate health care facilities, including information, counselling and services in family planning;

   (c) To benefit directly from social security programmes;

   (d) To obtain all types of training and education, formal and non-formal, including that relating to functional literacy, as well as, inter alia, the benefit of all community and extension services, in order to increase their technical proficiency;

(e) To organize self-help groups and co-operatives in order to obtain equal access to economic opportunities through employment or self-employment;

(f) To participate in all community activities;

(g) To have access to agricultural credit and loans, marketing facilities, appropriate technology and equal treatment in land and agrarian reform as well as in land resettlement schemes;

(h) To enjoy adequate living conditions, particularly in relation to housing, sanitation, electricity and water supply, transport and communications.

Part IV

Article 15

1. States Parties shall accord to women equality with men before the law.

2. States Parties shall accord to women, in civil matters, a legal capacity identical to that of men and the same opportunities to exercise that capacity. In particular, they shall give women equal rights to conclude contracts and to administer property and shall treat them equally in all stages of procedure in courts and tribunals.

3. States Parties agree that all contracts and all other private instruments of any kind with a legal effect which is directed at restricting the legal capacity of women shall be deemed null and void.

4. States Parties shall accord to men and women the same rights with regard to the law relating to the

movement of persons and the freedom to choose their residence and domicile.

Article 16

1. States Parties shall take all appropriate measures to eliminate discrimination against women in all matters relating to marriage and family relations and in particular shall ensure, on a basis of equality of men and women:

   (a) The same right to enter into marriage;

   (b) The same right freely to choose a spouse and to enter into marriage only with their free and full consent;

   (c) The same rights and responsibilities during marriage and at its dissolution;

   (d) The same rights and responsibilities as parents, irrespective of their marital status, in matters relating to their children; in all cases the interests of the children shall be paramount;

   (e) The same rights to decide freely and responsibly on the number and spacing of their children and to have access to the information, education and means to enable them to exercise these rights;

   (f) The same rights and responsibilities with regard to guardianship, wardship, trusteeship and adoption of children, or similar institutions where these concepts exist in national legislation; in all cases the interests of the children shall be paramount;

   (g) The same personal rights as husband and wife, including the right to choose a family name, a profession and an occupation;

(h) The same rights for both spouses in respect of the ownership, acquisition, management, administration, enjoyment and disposition of property, whether free of charge or for a valuable consideration.

2. The betrothal and the marriage of a child shall have no legal effect, and all necessary action, including legislation, shall be taken to specify a minimum age for marriage and to make the registration of marriages in an official registry compulsory.

Part V

Article 17

1. For the purpose of considering the progress made in the implementation of the present Convention, there shall be established a Committee on the Elimination of Discrimination against Women (hereinafter referred to as the Committee) consisting, at the time of entry into force of the Convention, of eighteen and, after ratification of or accession to the Convention by the thirty-fifth State Party, of twenty-three experts of high moral standing and competence in the field covered by the Convention. The experts shall be elected by States Parties from among their nationals and shall serve in their personal capacity, consideration being given to equitable geographical distribution and to the representation of the different forms of civilization as well as the principal legal systems.

2. The members of the Committee shall be elected by secret ballot from a list of persons nominated by

States Parties. Each Party may nominate one person from among its own nationals.

3. The initial election shall be held six months after the date of the entry into force of the present Convention. At least three months before the date of each election the Secretary-General of the United Nations shall address a letter to the States Parties inviting them to submit their nominations within two months. The Secretary-General shall prepare a list in alphabetical order of all persons thus nominated, indicating the States Parties which have nominated them, and shall submit it to the States Parties.

4. Elections of the members of the Committee shall be held at a meeting of States Parties convened by the Secretary-General at United Nations Headquarters. At that meeting, for which two thirds of the States Parties shall constitute a quorum, the persons elected to the Committee shall be those nominees who obtain the largest number of votes and an absolute majority of the votes of the representatives of States Parties present and voting.

5. The members of the Committee shall be elected for a term of four years. However, the terms of nine of the members elected at the first election shall expire at the end of two years; immediately after the first election the names of these nine members shall be chosen by lot by the Chairman of the Committee.

6. The election of the five additional members of the Committee shall be held in accordance with the provisions of paragraphs 2,3 and 4 of this article, following the thirty-fifth ratification or accession. The terms of two of the additional members elected on

this occasion shall expire at the end of two years, the names of these two members having been chosen by lot by the Chairman of the Committee.

7. For the filling of casual vacancies, the State Party whose expert has ceased to function as a member of the Committee shall appoint another expert from among its nationals, subject to the approval of the Committee.

8. The members of the Committee shall, with the approval of the General Assembly, receive emoluments from United Nations resources on such terms and conditions as the Assembly may decide, having regard to the importance of the Committee's responsibilities.

9. The Secretary-General of the United Nations shall provide the necessary staff and facilities for the effective performance of the functions of the Committee under the present Convention.

Article 18

1. States Parties undertake to submit to the Secretary-General of the United Nations, for consideration by the Committee, a report on the legislative, judicial, administrative or other measures which they have adopted to give effect to the provisions of the present Convention and on the progress made in this respect:

   (a) Within one year after the entry into force for the State concerned;

   (b) Thereafter at least every four years and further whenever the Committee so requests.

2. Reports may indicate factors and difficulties affecting the degree of fulfilment of obligations under the present Convention.

Article 19

1. The Committee shall adopt its own rules of procedure.
2. The Committee shall elect its officers for a term of two years.

Article 20

1. The Committee shall normally meet for a period of not more than two weeks annually in order to consider the reports submitted in accordance with article 18 of the present Convention.
2. The meetings of the Committee shall normally be held at United Nations Headquarters or at any other convenient place as determined by the Committee.

Article 21

1. The Committee shall, through the Economic and Social Council, report annually to the General Assembly of the United Nations on its activities and may make suggestions and general recommendations based on the examination of reports and information received from the States Parties. Such suggestions and general recommendations shall be included in the report of the Committee together with comments, if any, from States Parties.

2. The Secretary-General of the United Nations shall transmit the reports of the Committee to the Commission on the Status of Women for its information.

Article 22

The specialized agencies shall be entitled to be represented at the consideration of the implementation of such provisions of the present Convention as fall within the scope of their activities. The committee may invite the specialized agencies to submit reports on the implementation of the Convention in areas falling within the scope of their activities.

Part VI

Article 23

Nothing in the present Convention shall affect any provisions that are more conducive to the achievement of equality between men and women which may be contained:

(a) In the legislation of a State Party; or
(b) In any other international convention, treaty or agreement in force for that State.

Article 24

States Parties undertake to adopt all necessary measures at the national level aimed at achieving the full realization of the rights recognized in the present Convention.

Article 25

1. The present Convention shall be open for signature by all States.
2. The Secretary-General of the United Nations is designated as the depositary of the present Convention.
3. The present Convention is subject to ratification. Instruments of ratification shall be deposited with the Secretary-General of the United Nations.
4. The present Convention shall be open to accession by all States. Accession shall be effected by the deposit of an instrument of accession with the Secretary-General of the United Nations.

Article 26

1. A request for the revision of the present Convention may be made at any time by any State Party by means of a notification in writing addressed to the Secretary-General of the United Nations.
2. The General Assembly of the United Nations shall decide upon the steps, if any, to be taken in respect of such a request.

Article 27

1. The present Convention shall enter into force on the thirtieth day after the deposit with the Secretary-General of the United Nations of the twentieth instrument of ratification or accession.

2. For each State ratifying the present Convention or acceding to it after the deposit of the twentieth instrument of ratification or accession, the Convention shall enter into force on the thirtieth day after the date of the deposit of its own instrument of ratification or accession.

Article 28

1. The Secretary-General of the United Nations shall receive and circulate to all States the text of reservations made by States at the time of ratification or accession.
2. A reservation incompatible with the object and purpose of the present Convention shall not be permitted.
3. Reservations may be withdrawn at any time by notification to this effect addressed to the Secretary-General of the United Nations, who shall then inform all States thereof. Such notification shall take effect on the date on which it is received.

Article 29

1. Any dispute between two or more States Parties concerning the interpretation or application of the present Convention which is not settled by negotiation shall, at the request of one of them, be submitted to arbitration. If within six months from the date of the request for arbitration the parties are unable to agree on the organization of the arbitration, any one of those parties may refer the dispute to the

International Court of Justice by request in conformity with the statute of the Court.

2. Each State Party may at the time of signature or ratification of the present Convention or accession thereto declare that it does not consider itself bound by paragraph 1 of this article. The other States Parties shall not be bound by that paragraph with respect to any State Party which has made such a reservation.

3. Any State Party which has made a reservation in accordance with paragraph 2 of this article may at any time withdraw that reservation by notification to the Secretary-General of the United Nations.

Article 30

The present Convention, the Arabic, Chinese, English, French, Russian and Spanish texts of which are equally authentic, shall be deposited with the Secretary-General of the United Nations.

In Witness Whereof the undersigned, duly authorized, have signed the present Convention.

8

Convention on the Rights of the Child

(Adopted by the General Assembly of the United Nations on 20 November 1989)

Preamble

The States Parties to the present Convention,

Considering that, in accordance with the principles proclaimed in the Charter of the United Nations, recognition of the inherent dignity and of the equal and inalienable rights of all members of the human family is the foundation of freedom, justice and peace in the world,

Bearing in mind that the peoples of the United Nations, have, in the Charter, reaffirmed their faith in fundamental human rights and in the dignity and worth of the human person, and have determined to promote social progress and better standards of life in larger freedom,

Recognising that the United Nations has, in the Universal Declaration of Human Rights and in the International Covenants on Human Rights, proclaimed and agreed that everyone is entitled to all the rights and freedoms set forth therein, without distinction of any kind, such as race, colour, sex, language religion, political or other opinion, national or social origin, property, birth or other status,

Recalling that, in the Universal Declaration of Human Rights, the United Nations has proclaimed that childhood is entitled to special care and assistance,

Convinced that the family, as the fundamental group of society and the natural environment for the growth and well-being of all its members and particularly children, should be afforded the necessary protection and assistance so that it can fully assume its responsibilities within the community,

Recognising that the child, for the full and harmonious development of his or her personality, should grow up in a family environment, in an atmosphere of happiness, love and understanding,

Considering that the child should be fully prepared to live an individual life in society, and brought up in the spirit of the ideals proclaimed in the Charter of the United Nations, and in particular in the spirit of peace, dignity, tolerance, freedom, equality and solidarity,

Bearing in mind the need to extend particular care to the child has been stated in the Geneva Declaration of the Rights of the Child of 1924 and in the Declaration of the Rights of the Child adopted by the General Assembly on 20 November 1959 and recognised in the Universal Declaration of Human Rights, in the International Covenant on Civil and Political Rights (in particular in articles 23 and 24), in the International Covenant on Economic, Social and Cultural Rights (in particular in Article 10) and in the statutes and relevant instruments of specialised agencies and international organisations concerned with the welfare of children,

Bearing in mind as indicated in the Declaration of the Rights of the Child, "the child, by reason of his physical and mental immaturity, needs special safeguards and care, including appropriate legal protection, before as well as after birth",

Recalling the provisions of the Declaration on Social and Legal Principles relating to Protection and Welfare of Children, with Special Reference to Foster Placement and Adoption Nationally and Internationally; the United Nations Standard Minimum Rules for the Administration of Juvenile Justice (The Beijing Rules); and the Declaration on the Protection of Women and Children in Emergency and Armed Conflict,

Recognising that, in all countries in the world, there are children living in exceptionally difficult conditions, and the such children need special consideration,

Taking due account of the importance of the traditions and cultural values of each people for the protection and harmonious development of the child,

Recognising the importance of international cooperation for improving the living conditions of children in every country, in particular in the developing countries,

Have agreed as follows:

Part I

Article 1

For the purposes of the present Convention, a child means every human being below the age of eighteen years unless under the law applicable to the child, majority is attained earlier.

Article 2

1. States Parties shall respect and ensure the rights set forth in the present Convention to each child within their jurisdiction without discrimination of any kind, irrespective of the child's or his or her parent's or legal guardian's race, colour, sex, language, religion, political or other opinion, national ethnic or social origin, property, disability, birth or other status.

2. States Parties shall take all appropriate measures to ensure that the child is protected against all forms of discrimination or punishment on the basis of the status, activities, expressed opinions, or beliefs of the child's parents, legal guardians, or family members.

Article 3

1. In all actions concerning children, whether undertaken by public or private social welfare institutions, courts of law, administrative authorities or legislative bodies, the best interests of the child shall be a primary consideration.

2. States Parties undertake to ensure the child such protection and care as is necessary for his or her well-being, taking into account the rights and duties of his or her parents, legal guardians, or other individuals legally responsible for him or her, and to this end, shall take all appropriate legislative and administrative measures.

3. States Parties shall ensure that the institutions, services and facilities responsible for the care or protection of children shall conform with the standards established by competent authorities,

particularly in the areas of safety, health, in the number and suitability of their staff, as well as competent supervision.

Article 4

States Parties shall undertake all appropriate legislative, administrative, and other measures for the implementation of the rights recognised in the present Convention. With regard to economic, social and cultural rights, States Parties shall undertake such measures to the maximum extent of their available resources and, where needed, within the framework of international cooperation.

Article 5

States Parties shall respect the responsibilities, rights and duties of parents or, where applicable, the members of the extended family or community as provided for by local custom, legal guardians or other persons legally responsible for the child, to provide, in a manner consistent with the evolving capacities of the child, appropriate direction and guidance in the exercise by the child, appropriate direction and guidance in the exercise by the child of the rights recognised in the present Convention.

Article 6

1. States Parties recognise that every child has the inherent right to life.
2. States Parties shall ensure to the maximum extent possible the survival and development of the child.

Article 7

1. The child shall be registered immediately after birth and shall have the right from birth to a name, the right to acquire a nationality and, as far as possible, the right to know and be cared for by his or her parents.
2. States Parties shall ensure the implementation of these rights in accordance with their national law and their obligations under the relevant international instruments in this field, in particular where the child would otherwise be stateless.

Article 8

1. States Parties undertake to respect the right of the child to preserve his or her identity, including nationality, name and family relations as recognised by law without unlawful interference.
2. Where a child is illegally deprived of some or all of the elements of his or her identity, States Parties shall provide appropriate assistance and protection, with a view to re-establishing speedily his or her identity.

Article 9

1. States Parties shall ensure that a child shall not be separated from his or her parents against their will, except when competent authorities subject to judicial review determine, in accordance with applicable law and procedures, that such separation is necessary for the best interests of the child. Such determination may be necessary in a particular case such as one involving abuse or neglect of the child by the

parents, or one where the parents are living separately and a decision must be made as to the child's place of residence.

2. In any proceedings pursuant to paragraph 1 of the present Article, all interested parties shall be given an opportunity to participate in the proceeding and make their views known.

3. States Parties shall respect the right of the child who is separated from one or both parents to maintain personal relations and direct contact with both parents on a regular basis, except if it is contrary to the child's best interests.

4. Where such separation results from any action initiated by a States Party, such as the detention, imprisonment, exile, deportation or death (including death arising from any cause while the person is in the custody of the State) of one or both parents or of the child, that State Party shall, upon request, provide the parents, the child or, if appropriate, another member of the family with the essential information concerning the whereabouts of the absent member(s) of the family unless the provision of the information would be detrimental to the well-being of the child. States Parties shall further ensure that the submission of such a request shall of itself entail no adverse consequences for the person(s) concerned.

Article 10

1. In accordance with the obligation of States Parties under article 9, paragraph 1, applications by a child or his or her parents to enter or leave a State party

for the purpose of family reunification shall be dealt with by States Parties in a positive, humane and expeditious manner. States Parties shall further ensure that the submission of such a request shall entail no adverse consequences for the applicants and for the members of their family.

2. A child whose parents reside in different States shall have the right to maintain on a regular basis, save in exceptional circumstances personal relations and direct contacts with both parents. Towards that end and in accordance with the obligation of States Parties under article 9, paragraph 1, States Parties shall respect the right of the child and his or her parents to leave any country, including their own, and to enter their own country. The right to leave any country shall be subject only to such restrictions as are prescribed by law and which are necessary to protect the national security, public order (order public), public health or morals or the rights and freedoms of others and are consistent with the other rights recognised in the present Convention.

Article 11

1. States Parties shall take measures to combat the illicit transfer and non-return of children abroad.
2. To this end, States Parties shall promote the conclusion of bilateral or multilateral agreements or accession to existing agreements.

Article 12

1. States Parties shall assure to the child who is capable of forming his or her own views the right to express

those views freely in all matters affecting the child, the views of the child being given due weight in accordance with the age and maturity of the child.

2. For this purpose, the child shall in particular be provided the opportunity to be heard in any judicial and administrative proceedings affecting the child, either directly, or through a representative or an appropriate body, in a manner consistent with the procedural rules of national law.

Article 13

1. The child shall have the right to freedom of expression; this right shall include freedom to seek, receive and impart information and ideas of all kinds, regardless of frontiers, either orally, in writing or in print, in the form of art, or through any other media of the child's choice.
2. The exercise of this right may be subject to certain restrictions, but these shall only be such as are provided by law and are necessary:
   a) For respect of the rights or reputations of others, or
   b) For the protection of national security or of public order (order public), or of public health or morals.

Article 14

1. States Parties shall respect the right of the child to freedom of thought, conscience and religion.

2. States Parties shall respect the rights and duties of the parents and when applicable, legal guardians, to

provide direction to the child in the exercise of his or her right in a manner consistent with the evolving capacities of the child.

3. Freedom to manifest one's religion or beliefs may be subject only to such limitations as are prescribed by law and are necessary to protect public safety, order, health or morals, or the fundamental rights and freedoms of others.

Article 15

1. States Parties recognise the rights of the child to freedom of association and to freedom of peaceful assembly.

2. No restrictions may be placed on the exercise of these rights other than those imposed in conformity with the law and which are necessary in a democratic society in the interests of national security or public safety, public order (order public), the protection of public health or morals or the protection of the rights and freedoms of others.

Article 16

1. No child shall be subjected to arbitrary or unlawful interference with his or her privacy, family, home or correspondence, nor to unlawful attacks on his or her honour and reputation;

2. The child has the right to the protection of the law against such interference or attacks.

Article 17

States Parties recognise the important function performed by the mass media and shall ensure that the child has access to information and material from a diversity of national and international sources, especially those aimed at the promotion of his or her social, spiritual and moral well-being and physical and mental health. To this end, States Parties shall:

a) Encourage the mass media to disseminate information and material of social and cultural benefit to the child and in accordance with the spirit of Article 29;

b) Encourage international co-operation in the production, exchange and dissemination of such information and material from a diversity of cultural, national and international sources;

c) Encourage the production and dissemination of children's books;

d) Encourage the mass media to have particular regard to the linguistic needs of the child who belongs to a minority group or who is indigenous.

e) Encourage the development of appropriate guidelines for the protection of the child from information and material injurious to his or her well-being, bearing in mind the provisions of Articles 13 and 18.

Article 18

1. States Parties shall use their best efforts to ensure recognition of the principles that both parents have common responsibilities for the upbringing and

development of the child. Parents or, as the case may be, legal guardians, have the primary responsibility for the upbringing and development of the child. The best interests of the child will be their basic concern.

2. For the purpose of guaranteeing and promoting the rights set forth in the present Convention, States Parties shall render appropriate assistance to parents and legal guardians in the performance of their child-rearing responsibilities and shall ensure the development of institutions, facilities and services of the care of children.

3. States Parties shall take all appropriate measures to ensure that children of working parents have the right to benefit from child-care services and facilities for which they are eligible.

Article 19

1. States Parties shall take all appropriate legislative, administrative social and educational measures to protect the child from all forms of physical or mental violence, injury or abuse, neglect or negligent treatment, maltreatment or exploitation, including sexual abuse, while in the care of parent(s), legal guardian(s) or any other person who has the care of the child.

2. Such protective measures should, as appropriate, include effective procedures for the establishment of social programmes to provide necessary support for the child and for those who have the care of the child, as well as for other forms of prevention and for identification, reporting, referral, investigation, treatment and follow-up of instances of child

maltreatment described heretofore, and, as appropriate, for judicial involvement.

Article 20

1. A child temporarily or permanently deprived of his or her family environment, or in whose own best interests cannot be allowed to remain in that environment shall be entitled to special protection and assistance provided by the State.
2. States Parties shall in accordance with their national laws ensure alternative care for such a child.
3. Such care could include, *inter alia,* foster placement *kafalah of Islamic law,* adoption or if necessary placement in suitable institutions for the care of children. When considering solutions, due regard shall be paid to the desirability of continuity in a child's upbringing and to the child's ethnic, religious, cultural and linguistic background.

Article 21

States Parties that recognise and/or permit the system of adoption shall ensure that the best interests of the child shall be the paramount consideration and they shall:

a) Ensure that the adoption of a child is authorised only by competent authorities who determine, in accordance with applicable law and procedures and on the basis of all pertinent and reliable information, that the adoption is permissible in view of the child's status concerning parents, relatives and legal guardians and that, if required, the persons concerned have given their informed consent to the adoption on the basis of such counselling as may be necessary;

b) Recognised that inter-country adoption may be considered as an alternative means of child's care, if the child cannot be placed in a foster or an adoptive family or cannot in any suitable manner be cared for in the child's country of origin;

c) Ensure that the child concerned by inter-country adoption enjoys safeguards and standards equivalent to those existing in the case of national adoption;

d) Take all appropriate measures to ensure that, in inter-country adoption, the placement does not result in improper financial gain for those involved in it;

e) Promote, where appropriate, the objectives of the present article by concluding bilateral or multilateral arrangements or agreements, and endeavour, within this framework, to ensure that the placement of the child in another country is carried out by competent authorities or organs.

Article 22

1. States Parties shall take appropriate measures to ensure that a child who is seeking refugee status or who is considered a refugee in accordance with applicable international or domestic law and procedures shall, whether unaccompanied or accompanied by his or her parents or by any other person, receive appropriate protection and humanitarian assistance in the enjoyment of applicable rights set forth in the present Convention and in other international human rights or humanitarian instruments to which the said States are Parties.

2. For this purpose, States Parties shall provide, as they consider appropriate, co-operation in any efforts by the United Nations and other competent inter-governmental organisations or non-governmental organisations co-operating with the United Nations to protect and assist such a child and to trace the parents or other members of the family of any refugee child in order to obtain information necessary for reunification with his or her family. In cases where no parents or other members of the family can be found, the child shall be accorded the same protection as any other child permanently or temporarily deprived of his or her family environment for any reason, as set forth in the present Convention.

Article 23

1. States Parties recognise that a mentally or physically disabled child should enjoy a full and decent life, in conditions which ensure dignity, promote self-reliance and facilitate the child's active participation in the community.
2. States Parties recognise the right of the disabled child to special care and shall encourage and ensure the extension, subject to available resources, to the eligible child and those responsible for his or her care, of assistance for which application is made and which is appropriate to the child's condition and to the circumstances of the parents or others caring for the child.
3. Recognising the special needs of a disabled child, assistances extended in accordance with paragraph 2

of the present article shall be provided free of charge, whenever possible, taking into account the financial resources of the parents or others caring for the child, and shall be designed to ensure that the disabled child has effective access to and receives education, training, health care services, rehabilitation services, preparation for employment and recreation opportunities in a manner conducive to the child's achieving the fullest possible social integration and individual development, including his or her cultural and spiritual development.

4. States Parties shall promote, in the spirit of international cooperation, the exchange of appropriate information in the field of preventive health care and of medical psychological and functional treatment of disabled children, including dissemination of and access to information concerning methods of rehabilitation, education and vocational services, with the aim of enabling States Parties to improve their capabilities and skills and to widen their experience in these areas. In this regard, particular account shall be taken of the needs of developing countries.

Article 24

1. States Parties recognise the right of the child to the enjoyment of the highest attainable standard of health and to facilities for the treatment of illness and rehabilitation of health. States Parties shall strive to ensure that no child is deprived of his or her right of access to such health care services.

2. States Parties shall pursue full implementation of this right and, in particular, shall take appropriate measures:

a) To diminish infant and child mortality;

b) To ensure the provision of necessary medical assistance and health care to all children with emphasis on the development of primary health care;

c) To combat disease and malnutrition, including within the framework of primary health care, through, *inter alia*, the application of readily available technology and through the provision of adequate nutritious foods and clean drinking water, taking into consideration the dangers and risks of environmental pollution;

d) To ensure appropriate pre-natal and post-natal health care for mothers;

e) To ensure that all segments of society, in particular parents and children, are informed, have access to education and are supported in the use of basic knowledge of child health and nutrition, the advantages of breastfeeding, hygiene and environmental sanitation and the prevention of accidents;

f) To develop preventive health care, guidance for parents and family planning education and services.

3. States Parties shall take all effective and appropriate measures with a view to abolishing traditional practices prejudicial to the health of children.

4. States Parties undertake to promote and encourage international cooperation with a view to achieving progressively the full realisation of the right recognised in the present article. In this regard,

particular account shall be taken of the needs of developing countries.

Article 25

States Parties recognise the right of a child who has been placed by the competent authorities for the purposes of care, protection or treatment of his or her physical or mental health, to a periodic review of the treatment provided to the child and all other circumstances relevant to his or her placement.

Article 26

1. States Parties shall recognise for every child the right to benefit from social security, including social insurance, and shall take the necessary measures to achieve the full realisation of this right in accordance with their national law.
2. The benefits should, where appropriate, be granted, taking into account the resources and the circumstances of the child and persons having responsibility for the maintenance of the child, as well as any other consideration relevant to an application for benefits made by or on behalf of the child.

Article 27

1. States Parties recognise the right of every child to a standard of living adequate for the child's physical, mental, spiritual, moral and social development.

2. The parent(s) or others responsible for the child have the primary responsibility to secure, within their abilities and financial capacities, the conditions of living necessary for the child's development;

3. States Parties, in accordance with national conditions and within their means, shall take appropriate measures to assist parents and others responsible for the child to implement this right and shall in case of need provide material assistance and support programmes, particularly with regard to nutrition, clothing and housing.

4. States Parties shall take all appropriate measures to secure the recovery of maintenance for the child from the parents of other persons having financial responsibility for the child, both within the State Party and from abroad. In particular, where the person having financial responsibility for the child lives in a State different from that of the child, States Parties shall promote the accession to international agreements of the conclusion of such agreements, as well as the making of other appropriate arrangements.

Article 28

1. States Parties recognise the right of the child to education, and with a view to achieving this right progressively and on the basis of equal opportunity, they shall, in particular:

   a) Make primary education compulsory and available free to all;

   b) Encourage the development of different forms of secondary education, including general and vocational education, make them available and accessible to every child, and take appropriate measures such as the introduction of free education and offering financial assistance in case of need;

c) Make higher education accessible to all on the basis of capacity by every appropriate means;

d) Make educational and vocational information and guidance available and accessible to all children;

e) Take measures to encourage regular attendance at schools and the reduction of dropout rates.

2. States Parties shall take all appropriate measures to ensure that school discipline is administered in a manner consistent with the child's human dignity and in conformity with the present Convention.

3. States Parties shall promote and encourage international cooperation in matters relating to education, in particular with a view to contributing to the elimination of ignorance and illiteracy throughout the world and facilitating access to scientific and technical knowledge and modern teaching methods. In this regard, particular account shall be taken of the needs of developing countries.

Article 29

1. States Parties agree that the education on the child shall be directed to:

a) The development of the child's personality, talents and mental and physical abilities to their fullest potential;

b) The development of respect for human rights and fundamental freedoms, and for the principles enshrined in the Charter of the United Nations.

c) The development of respect for the child's parents, his or her own cultural identity, language and values, for the national values of the country in which the child is living, the country from which he or she may originate, and for civilisations different from his or her own;

d) The preparation of the child for responsible life in a free society, in the spirit of understanding, peace tolerance equality of sexes, and friendship among all peoples, ethnic, national and religious groups and persons of indigenous origin;

e) The development of respect for the natural environment.

2. No part of the present Article or article 28 shall be construed so as to interfere with the liberty of individuals and bodies to establish and direct educational institutions, subject always to the observance of the principle set forth in paragraph 1 of the present article and to the requirements that the education given in such institutions shall confirm to such minimum standards as may be laid down by the State.

Article 30

In those States in which ethnic, religious or linguistic minorities or persons of indigenous origin exist, a child belonging to such a minority or who is indigenous shall not be denied the right, in community with other members of his or her group, to enjoy his or her own culture, to profess and practise his or her own religion, or to use his or her own language.

Article 31

1. States Parties recognise the right of the child to rest and leisure, to engage in play and recreational activities appropriate to the age of the child and to participate freely in cultural life and the arts.
2. States Parties shall respect and promote the right of the child to participate fully in cultural and artistic life and shall encourage the provision of appropriate and equal opportunities for cultural, artistic, recreational and leisure activity.

Article 32

1. States Parties recognise the right of the child to be protected from economic exploitation and from performing any work that is likely to be hazardous or to interfere with the child's education, or to be harmful to the child's health or physical, mental, spiritual, moral or social development.
2. States Parties shall take legislative, administrative, social and educational measures to ensure the implementation of the present article. To this end, and having regard to the relevant provisions of other international instruments, States Parties shall in particular:

    a) Provide for a minimum age or minimum ages for admission to employment;

b) Provide for appropriate regulation of the hours and conditions of employment; and

c) Provide for appropriate penalties or other sanctions to ensure the effective enforcement of the present article.

Article 33

States Parties shall take all appropriate measures, including legislative, administrative, social and educational measures, to protect children from the illicit use of narcotic drugs and psychotropic substances as defined in the relevant international treaties, and to prevent the use of children in the illicit production and trafficking of such substances.

Article 34

States Parties undertake to protect the child from all forms of sexual exploitation and sexual abuse. For these purposes, States Parties shall in particular take all appropriate national, bilateral and multilateral measures to prevent:

a) The inducement or coercion of a child to engage in any unlawful sexual activity;

b) The exploitative use of children in prostitution or other unlawful sexual practices; and

c) The exploitative use of children in pornographic performances and materials.

Article 35

States Parties shall take all appropriate national, bilateral and multilateral measures to prevent the abduction of the sale of or traffic in children for any purpose or in any form.

Article 36

States Parties shall protect the child against all other forms of exploitation prejudicial to any aspects of the child's welfare.

Article 37

States Parties shall ensure that:

a) No child shall be subjected to torture or other cruel, inhuman or degrading treatment or punishment. Neither capital punishment nor life imprisonment without possibility of release shall be imposed for offences committed by persons below eighteen years of age;

b) No child shall be deprived of his or her liberty unlawfully or arbitrarily. The arrest, detention or imprisonment of a child shall be in conformity with the law and shall be used only as a measure of last resort and for the shortest appropriate period of time;

c) Every child deprived of liberty shall be treated with humanity and respect for the inherent dignity of the human person, and in a manner which takes into account the needs of persons of his or her age. In particular, every child deprived of liberty shall be separated from adults unless it is considered in the child's best interest not to do so and shall have the right to maintain contact with his or her family through correspondence and visits, save in exceptional circumstances; and

d) Every child deprived of his or her liberty shall have the right to prompt access to legal and other appropriate assistance, as well as the right to challenge the legality of the deprivation of his or her liberty before a court or other competent, independent and impartial authority, and to a prompt decision on any such action.

Article 38

1. States Parties undertake to respect and to ensure respect for rules of international humanitarian law applicable to them in armed conflicts which are relevant to the child.

2. States Parties shall take all feasible measures to ensure that persons who have not attained the age of fifteen years do not take a direct part in hostilities.

3. States Parties shall refrain from recruiting any person who has not attained the age of fifteen years into their armed forces. In recruiting among those persons who have attained the age of fifteen years but who have not attained the age of eighteen years, States Parties shall endeavour to give priority to those who are oldest.

4. In accordance with their obligations under international humanitarian law to protect the civilian population in armed conflicts, States Parties shall take all feasible measures to ensure protection and

care of children who are affected by an armed conflict.

Article 39

States Parties shall take all appropriate measures to promote physical and psychological recovery and social reintegration of a child victim of: any form of neglect, exploitation, or abuse; torture or any other form of cruel, inhuman or degrading treatment or punishment; or armed conflicts. Such recovery and reintegration shall take place in an environment which fosters the health, self-respect and dignity of the child.

Article 40

1. States Parties recognise the right of every child alleged as, accused of, or recognised as having infringed the penal law to be treated in a manner consistent with the promotion of the child's sense of dignity and worth, which reinforces the child's respect for the human rights and fundamental freedoms of others and which takes into account the child's age and the desirability of promoting the child's reintegration and the child's assuming a constructive role in society.

2. To this end, and having regard to the relevant provisions of international instruments, States Parties shall, in particular, ensure that:

   a) No child shall be alleged as, be accused of, or recognised as having infringed the penal law by reason of acts or omissions that were not prohibited by national or international law at the time they were committed;

b) Every child alleged as or accused of having infringed the penal law has at least the following guarantees:

i) To be presumed innocent until proven guilty according to law;

ii) To be informed promptly and directly of the charges against him or her, and, if appropriate, through his or her parents of legal guardians, and to have legal or other appropriate assistance in the preparation and presentation of his or her defence;

iii) To have the matter determined without delay by a competent, independent and impartial authority or judicial body in a fair hearing according to law, in the presence of legal or other appropriate assistance and, unless it is considered not to be in the best interest of the child, in particular, taking into account his or her age or situation, his or her parents or legal guardians;

iv) Not to be compelled to give testimony or to confess guilt; to examine or have examined adverse witnesses and to obtain the participation and examination of witnesses on his or her behalf under conditions of equality;

v) If considered to have infringed the penal law to have this decision and any measures imposed in consequence thereof reviewed by a higher competent, independent and impartial authority or judicial body according to law;

vi) To have the free assistance of an interpreter if the child cannot understand or speak the language used; and

vii) To have his or her privacy fully respected at all stages of the proceedings.

3. States Parties shall seek to promote the establishment of laws, procedures, authorities and institutions specifically applicable to children alleged as, accused of or recognised as having infringed the penal law, and, in particular:

   a) The establishment of a minimum age below which children shall be presumed not to have the capacity to infringe the penal law; and

   b) Whenever appropriate and desirable measures for dealing with such children without resorting to judicial proceedings, providing that human rights and legal safeguards are fully respected.

4. A variety of dispositions, such as care, guidance and supervision orders; counselling; probation; foster care; education and vocational training programmes and other alternatives to institutional care shall be available to ensure that children are dealt with in a manner appropriate to their well being and proportionate both to their circumstances and the offence.

Article 41

Nothing in the present Convention shall affect any provisions which are more conducive to the realisation of the rights of the child and which may be contained in:

a) The law of a State Party; or

b) International law in force for that State.

Part II

Article 42

States Parties undertake to make the principles and provisions of the Convention widely known, by appropriate and active means, to adults and children alike.

Article 43

1. For the purpose of examining the progress made by States Parties in achieving the realisation of the obligations undertaken in the present Convention, there shall be established a Committee in the Rights of the Child, which shall carry out the functions hereinafter provided.
2. The Committee shall consist of ten experts of high moral standing and recognised competence in the field covered by this Convention. The members of the Committee shall be elected by States Parties from among their nationals and shall serve in their personal capacity, consideration being given to equitable geographical distribution, as well as to the principal legal systems.
3. The members of the Committee shall be elected by secret ballot from a list of persons nominated by States Parties. Each State Party may nominate one person from among its own nationals.
4. The initial election to the Committee shall be held no later than six months after the date of the entry into force of the present Convention and thereafter every

second year. At least four months before the date of each election, the Secretary-General of the United Nations shall address a letter to States Parties inviting them to submit their nominations within two months. The Secretary-General shall subsequently prepare a list in alphabetical order of all persons thus nominated, indicating States Parties which have nominated them, and shall submit it to the States Parties to the present Convention.

5. The elections shall be held at meetings of States Parties convened by the Secretary-General at United Nations Headquarters. At those meetings, for which two thirds of States Parties shall constitute a quorum, the persons elected to the Committee shall be those who obtain the largest number of votes and an absolute majority of the votes of the representatives of States Parties present and voting.

6. The members of the Committee shall be elected for a term of four years. They shall be eligible for re-election if renominated. The term of five of the members elected at the first election, shall expire at the end of two years; immediately after the first election the names of these five members shall be chosen by lot by the Chairman of the meeting.

7. If a member of the Committee dies or resigns or declares that for any other cause he or she can no longer perform the duties of the Committee, the State Party which nominated the member shall appoint another expert from among its nationals to serve for the remainder of the term, subject to the approval of the Committee.

8. The Committee shall establish its own rules of procedure.

9. The Committee shall elect its officers for a period of two years.

10. The meetings of the Committee shall normally be held at United Nations Headquarters or at any other convenient place as determined by the Committee. The Committee shall normally meet annually. The duration of the meetings of the Committee shall be determined, and reviewed, subject to the approval of the General Assembly.

11. The Secretary-General of the United Nations shall provide the necessary staff and facilities for the United Nations shall provide the necessary staff and facilities for the effective performance of the functions of the Committee under the present Convention.

12. With the approval of the General Assembly, the members of the Committee established under the present Convention shall receive emoluments from United Nations resources on such terms and conditions as the Assembly may decide.

Article 44

1. States Parties undertake to submit to the Committee, through the Secretary-General of the United Nations, reports on the measures they have adopted which give effect to the rights recognised herein and on the progress made on the enjoyment of those rights:

   a) Within two years of the entry into force of the Convention for the State Party concerned; and

   b) Thereafter every five years.

2. Reports made under the present article shall indicate factors and difficulties, if any affecting the degree of fulfilment of the obligations under the present Convention. Reports shall also contain sufficient information to provide the Committee with a comprehensive understanding of the implementation of the Convention in the country concerned.

3. A State Party which has submitted a comprehensive initial report to the Committee need not, in its subsequent reports submitted in accordance with paragraph 1 (b) of the present article, repeat basic information previously provided.

4. The Committee may request from States Parties further information relevant to the implementation of the Convention.

5. The Committee shall submit to the General Assembly, through the Economic and Social Council, every two years, reports on its activities.

6. States Parties shall make their reports widely available to the public in their own countries.

Article 45

In order to foster the effective implementation of the Convention and to encourage international cooperation in the field covered by the Convention:

a) The specialised agencies, the United Nations Children's Fund, and other United Nations organs shall be entitled to be represented at the consideration of the implementation of such provisions of the present Convention as fall within the scope of their mandate. The Committee may invite the specialised agencies, the United Nations Children's Fund and other competent bodies as it may consider appropriate to provide expert advice on the implementation of the Convention in areas falling within the scope of their respective mandates. The Committee may invite the specialised agencies, the United Nations Children's Fund, and other United Nations organs to submit reports on the implementation of the Convention in areas falling within the scope of their activities;

b) The Committee shall transmit, as it may consider appropriate to the specialised agencies, the United Nations Children's Fund and other competent bodies, any reports from States Parties that contain a request, or indicate a need, for technical advice or assistance, along with the Committee's observations and suggestions, if any, on these requests or indications;

c) The Committee may recommend to the General Assembly to request the Secretary-General to undertake on its behalf studies on specific issues relating to the rights of the child;

d) The Committee may make suggestions and general recommendations based on information received pursuant to articles 44 and 45 of the present Convention. Such suggestions and general recommen-dations shall be transmitted to any State Party concerned and reported to the General Assembly, together with comments, if any, from States Parties.

Part III

Article 46

The present Convention shall be open for signature by all States.

Article 47

The present Convention is subject to ratification. Instruments of ratification shall be deposited with the Secretary-General of the United Nations.

Article 48

The present Convention shall remain open for accession by any State. The instruments of accession shall be deposited with the Secretary-General of the United Nations.

Article 49

1. The present Convention shall enter into force on the thirtieth day following the date of deposit with the Secretary-General of the United Nations of the twentieth instrument of ratification or accession.
2. For each State ratifying or acceding to the Convention after the deposit of the twentieth instrument of ratification or accession, the Convention shall enter into force on the thirtieth day after the deposit by such State of its instrument of ratification or accession.

Article 50

1. Any State Party may propose an amendment and file it with the Secretary-General of the United Nations. The Secretary-General shall thereupon communicate the proposed amendment to States Parties, with a request that they indicate whether they favour a conference of States Parties for the purpose of considering and voting upon the proposal. In the event that, within four months from the date of such communication, at least one third of the States Parties favour such a conference, the Secretary-General shall convene the conference under the auspices of the United Nations. Any amendment adopted by a majority of States Parties present and voting at the conference shall be submitted to the General Assembly for approval.

2. An amendment adopted in accordance with paragraph 1 of the present article shall enter into force when it has been approved by the General Assembly of the United Nations and accepted by a two-thirds majority of States Parties.

3. When an amendment enters into force, it shall be binding on those States Parties which have accepted it, other States Parties still being bound by the provisions of the present Convention and any earlier amendments which they have accepted.

Article 51

1. The Secretary-General of the United Nations shall receive and circulate to all States the text of reservations made by States at the time of ratification or accession.

2. A reservation incompatible with the object and purpose of the present Convention shall not be permitted.
3. Reservations may be withdrawn at any time by notification to that effect addressed to the Secretary-General of the United Nations, who shall then inform all states. Such notification shall take effect on the date on which it is received by the Secretary-General.

Article 52

A State Party may denounce the present Convention by written notification to the Secretary-General of the United Nations. Denunciation becomes effective one year after the date of receipt of the notification by the Secretary-General.

Article 53

The Secretary-General of the United Nations is designated as the depositary of the present Convention.

Article 54

The original of the present Convention, of which the Arabic, Chinese, English French, Russian and Spanish text are equally authentic, shall be deposited with the Secretary-General of the United Nations.

In Witness Whereof the undersigned plenipotentiaries, being duly authorised thereto by their respective Governments have signed the present Convention.

9

Convention Relating to the Status of Refugees

(189 U.N.T.S. 150, entered into force April 22, 1954)

Preamble

The High Contracting Parties,

Considering that the Charter of the United Nations and the Universal Declaration of Human Rights approved on 10 December 1948 by the General Assembly have affirmed the principle that human beings shall enjoy fundamental rights and freedoms without discrimination,

Considering that the United Nations has, on various occasions, manifested its profound concern for refugees and endeavoured to assure refugees the widest possible exercise of these fundamental rights and freedoms,

Considering that it is desirable to revise and consolidate previous international agreements relating to the status of refugees and to extend the scope of and the protection accorded by such instruments by means of a new agreement,

Considering that the grant of asylum may place unduly heavy burdens on certain countries, and that a satisfactory solution of a problem of which the United Nations has recognized the international- scope and nature cannot therefore be achieved without international co-operation,

Expressing the wish that all States, recognizing the social and humanitarian nature of the problem of refugees, will do everything within their power to prevent this problem from becoming a cause of tension between States,

Noting that the United Nations High Commissioner for Refugees is charged with the task of supervising international conventions providing for the protection of refugees, and recognizing that the effective co-ordination of measures taken to deal with this problem will depend upon the co-operation of States with the High Commissioner,

Have agreed as follows:

Chapter I: General Provisions

Article 1. - Definition of the term "refugee"

A. For the purposes of the present Convention, the term "refugee,, shall apply to any person who:

   (1) Has been considered a refugee under the Arrangements of 12 May 1926 and 30 June 1928

or under the Conventions of 28 October 1933 and 10 February 1938, the Protocol of 14 September 1939 or the Constitution of the International Refugee Organization;

Decisions of non-eligibility taken by the International Refugee Organization during the period of its activities shall not prevent the status of refugee being accorded to persons who fulfil the conditions of paragraph 2 of this section;

(2) As a result of events occurring before I January 1951 and owing to well-founded fear of being persecuted for reasons of race, religion, nationality, membership of a particular social group or political opinion, is outside the country of his nationality and is unable, or owing to such fear, is unwilling to avail himself of the protection of that country; or who, not having a nationality and being outside the country of his former habitual residence as a result of such events, is unable or, owing to such fear, is unwilling to return to it.

In the case of a person who has more than one nationality, the term "the country of his nationality" shall mean each of the countries of which he is a national, and a person shall not be deemed to be lacking the protection of the country of his nationality if, without any valid reason based on well-founded fear, he has not availed himself of the protection of one of the countries of which he is a national.

B.

(1) For the purposes of this Convention, the words "events occurring before I January 1951" in

article 1, section A, shall be understood to mean either (a) "events occurring in Europe before I January 1951"; or (b) "events occurring in Europe or elsewhere before I January 1951"; and each Contracting State shall make a declaration at the time of signature, ratification or accession, specifying which of these meanings it applies for the purpose of its obligations under this Convention.

(2) Any Contracting State which has adopted alternative (a) may at any time extend its obligations by adopting alternative (b) by means of a notification addressed to the Secretary-General of the United Nations.

C. This Convention shall cease to apply to any person falling under the terms of section A if:

(1) He has voluntarily re-availed himself of the protection of the country of his nationality; or

(2) Having lost his nationality, he has voluntarily reacquired it; or

(3) He has acquired a new nationality, and enjoys the protection of the country of his new nationality; or

(4) He has voluntarily re-established himself in the country which he left or outside which he remained owing to fear of persecution; or

(5) He can no longer, because the circumstances in connection with which he has been recognized as a refugee have ceased to exist, continue to refuse to avail himself of the protection of the country of his nationality;

Provided that this paragraph shall not apply to a refugee falling under section A (I) of this article who is able to invoke compelling reasons arising out of previous persecution for refusing to avail himself of the protection of the country of nationality;

(6) Being a person who has no nationality he is, because the circumstances in connection with which he has been recognized as a refugee have ceased to exist, able to return to the country of his former habitual residence;

Provided that this paragraph shall not apply to a refugee falling under section A (I) of this article who is able to invoke compelling reasons arising out of previous persecution for refusing to return to the country of his former habitual residence.

D. This Convention shall not apply to persons who are at present receiving from organs or agencies of the United Nations other than the United Nations High Commissioner for Refugees protection or assistance.

When such protection or assistance has ceased for any reason, without the position of such persons being definitively settled in accordance with the relevant resolutions adopted by the General Assembly of the United Nations, these persons shall ipso facto be entitled to the benefits of this Convention.

E. This Convention shall not apply to a person who is recognized by the competent authorities of the country in which he has taken residence as having the rights and obligations which are attached to the possession of the nationality of that country.

F. The provisions of this Convention shall not apply to any person with respect to whom there are serious reasons for considering that.

(a) He has committed a crime against peace, a war crime, or a crime against humanity, as defined in the international instruments drawn up to make provision in respect of such crimes;

(b) He has committed a serious non-political crime outside the country of refuge prior to his admission to that country as a refugee;

(c) He has been guilty of acts contrary to the purposes and principles of the United Nations.

Article 2. - General obligations

Every refugee has duties to the country in which he finds himself, which require in particular that he conform to its laws and regulations as well as to measures taken for the maintenance of public order.

Article 3. - Non-discrimination

The Contracting States shall apply the provisions of this Convention to refugees without discrimination as to race, religion or country of origin.

Article 4. - Religion

The Contracting States shall accord to refugees within their territories treatment at least as favourable as that accorded to their nationals with respect to freedom to practise their religion and freedom as regards the religious education of their children.

Article 5. - Rights granted apart from this Convention

Nothing in this Convention shall be deemed to impair any rights and benefits granted by a Contracting State to refugees apart from this Convention.

Article 6. - The term "in the same circumstances"

For the purposes of this Convention, the term "in the same circumstances,, implies that any requirements (including requirements as to length and conditions of sojourn or residence) which the particular individual would have to fulfil for the enjoyment of the right in question, if he were not a refugee, must be fulfilled by him, with the exception of requirements which by their nature a refugee is incapable of fulfilling.

Article 7. - Exemption from reciprocity

1. Except where this Convention contains more favourable provisions, a Contracting State shall accord to refugees the same treatment as is accorded to aliens generally.
2. After a period of three years' residence, all refugees shall enjoy exemption from legislative reciprocity in the territory of the Contracting States.
3. Each Contracting State shall continue to accord to refugees the rights and benefits to which they were already entitled, in the absence of reciprocity, at the

date of entry into force of this Convention for that State.

4. The Contracting States shall consider favourably the possibility of according to refugees, in the absence of reciprocity, rights and benefits beyond those to which they are entitled according to paragraphs 2 and 3, and to extending exemption from reciprocity to refugees who do not fulfil the conditions provided for in paragraphs 2 and 3.

5. The provisions of paragraphs 2 and 3 apply both to the rights and benefits referred to in articles 13, 18, 19, 21 and 22 of this Convention and to rights and benefits for which this Convention does not provide.

Article 8. - Exemption from exceptional measures

With regard to exceptional measures which may be taken against the person, property or interests of nationals of a foreign State, the Contracting States shall not apply such measures to a refugee who is formally a national of the said State solely on account of such nationality. Contracting States which, under their legislation, are prevented from applying the general principle expressed in this article, shall, in appropriate cases, grant exemptions in favour of such refugees.

Article 9. - Provisional measures

Nothing in this Convention shall prevent a Contracting State, in time of war or other grave and exceptional circumstances, from taking provisionally measures which it considers to be essential to the national security in the case of a particular person, pending a determination by the Contracting State that that person is in fact a refugee and that the continuance of such measures is necessary in his case in the interests of national security.

Article 10. - Continuity of residence

1. Where a refugee has been forcibly displaced during the Second World War and removed to the territory of a Contracting State, and is resident there, the period of such enforced sojourn shall be considered to have been lawful residence within that territory.
2. Where a refugee has been forcibly displaced during the Second World War from the territory of a Contracting State and has, prior to the date of entry into force of this Convention, returned there for the purpose of taking up residence, the period of residence before and after such enforced displacement shall be regarded as one uninterrupted period for any purposes for which uninterrupted residence is required.

Article 11. - Refugee seamen

In the case of refugees regularly serving as crew members on board a ship flying the flag of a Contracting State, that State shall give sympathetic consideration to their establishment on its territory and the issue of travel documents to them or their temporary admission to its territory particularly with a view to facilitating their establishment in another country.

Chapter II: Judicial Status

Article 12. - Personal status

1. The personal status of a refugee shall be governed by the law of the country of his domicile or, if he has no domicile, by the law of the country of his residence.
2. Rights previously acquired by a refugee and dependent on personal status, more particularly rights attaching to marriage, shall be respected by a Contracting State, subject to compliance, if this be necessary, with the formalities required by the law of that State, provided that the right in question is one which would have been recognized by the law of that State had he not become a refugee.

Article 13. - Movable and immovable property

The Contracting States shall accord to a refugee treatment as favourable as possible and, in any event, not less favourable than that accorded to aliens generally in the same circumstances, as regards the acquisition of movable and immovable property and other rights pertaining thereto, and to leases and other contracts relating to movable and immovable property.

Article 14. - Artistic rights and industrial property

In respect of the protection of industrial property, such as inventions, designs or models, trade marks, trade names, and of rights in literary, artistic and scientific works, a refugee shall be accorded in the country in which he has his habitual residence the same protection as is accorded to nationals of that country. In the territory of any other

Contracting States, he shall be accorded the same protection as is accorded in that territory to nationals of the country in which he has his habitual residence.

Article 15. - Right of association

As regards non-political and non-profit-making associations and trade unions the Contracting States shall accord to refugees lawfully staying in their territory the most favourable treatment accorded to nationals of a foreign country, in the same circumstances.

Article 16. - Access to courts

1. A refugee shall have free access to the courts of law on the territory of all Contracting States.
2. A refugee shall enjoy in the Contracting State in which he has his habitual residence the same treatment as a national in matters pertaining to access to the courts, including legal assistance and exemption from cautio judicatum solvi.
3. A refugee shall be accorded in the matters referred to in paragraph 2 in countries other than that in which he has his habitual residence the treatment granted to a national of the country of his habitual residence.

Chapter III: Gaiful Employment

Article 17. - Wage-earning employment

1. The Contracting States shall accord to refugees lawfully staying in their territory the most favourable treatment accorded to nationals of a foreign country

in the same circumstances, as regards the right to engage in wage-earning employment.

2. In any case, restrictive measures imposed on aliens or the employment of aliens for the protection of the national labour market shall not be applied to a refugee who was already exempt from them at the date of entry into force of this Convention for the Contracting State concerned, or who fulfils one of the following conditions:

   (a) He has completed three years' residence in the country;

   (b) He has a spouse possessing the nationality of the country of residence. A refugee may not invoke the benefit of this provision if he has abandoned his spouse;

   (c) He has one or more children possessing the nationality of the country of residence.

3. The Contracting States shall give sympathetic consideration to assimilating the rights of all refugees with regard to wage-earning employment to those of nationals, and in particular of those refugees who have entered their territory pursuant to programmes of labour recruitment or under immigration schemes.

Article 18. - Self-employment

The Contracting States shall accord to a refugee lawfully in their territory treatment as favourable as possible and, in any event, not less favourable than that accorded to aliens generally in the same circumstances, as regards the right to engage on his own account in agriculture, industry, handicrafts and commerce and to establish commercial and industrial companies.

Article 19. - Liberal professions

1. Each Contracting State shall accord to refugees lawfully staying in their territory who hold diplomas recognized by the competent authorities of that State, and who are desirous of practising a liberal profession, treatment as favourable as possible and, in any event, not less favourable than that accorded to aliens generally in the same circumstances.
2. The Contracting States shall use their best endeavours consistently with their laws and constitutions to secure the settlement of such refugees in the territories, other than the metropolitan territory, for whose international relations they are responsible.

Chapter IV: Welfare

Article 20. - Rationing

Where a rationing system exists, which applies to the population at large and regulates the general distribution of products in short supply, refugees shall be accorded the same treatment as nationals.

Article 21. - Housing

As regards housing, the Contracting States, in so far as the matter is regulated by laws or regulations or is subject to the control of public authorities, shall accord to refugees lawfully staying in their territory treatment as favourable as possible and, in any event, not less favourable than that accorded to aliens generally in the same circumstances.

Article 22. - Public education

1. The Contracting States shall accord to refugees the same treatment as is accorded to nationals with respect to elementary education.
2. The Contracting States shall accord to refugees treatment as favourable as possible, and, in any event, not less favourable than that accorded to aliens generally in the same circumstances, with respect to education other than elementary education and, in particular, as regards access to studies, the recognition of foreign school certificates, diplomas and degrees, the remission of fees and charges and the award of scholarships.

Article 23. - Public relief

The Contracting States shall accord to refugees lawfully staying in their territory the same treatment with respect to public relief and assistance as is accorded to their nationals.

Article 24. - Labour legislation and social security

1. The Contracting States shall accord to refugees lawfully staying in their territory the same treatment as is accorded to nationals in respect of the following matters;

   (a) In so far as such matters are governed by laws or regulations or are subject to the control of administrative authorities: remuneration, including family allowances where these form part of remuneration, hours of work, overtime arrangements, holidays with pay, restrictions on home work, minimum age of employment, apprenticeship and training, women's work and the work of young persons, and the enjoyment of the benefits of collective bargaining;

(b) Social security (legal provisions in respect of employment injury, occupational diseases, maternity, sickness, disability, old age, death, unemployment, family responsibilities and any other contingency which, according to national laws or regulations, is covered by a social security scheme), subject to the following limitations:

(i) There may be appropriate arrangements for the maintenance of acquired rights and rights in course of acquisition;

(ii) National laws or regulations of the country of residence may prescribe special arrangements concerning benefits or portions of benefits which are payable wholly out of public funds, and concerning allowances paid to persons who do not fulfil the contribution conditions prescribed for the award of a normal pension.

2. The right to compensation for the death of a refugee resulting from employment injury or from occupational disease shall not be affected by the fact that the residence of the beneficiary is outside the territory of the Contracting State.

3. The Contracting States shall extend to refugees the benefits of agreements concluded between them, or which may be concluded between them in the future, concerning the maintenance of acquired rights and

rights in the process of acquisition in regard to social security, subject only to the conditions which apply to nationals of the States signatory to the agreements in question.

4. The Contracting States will give sympathetic consideration to extending to refugees so far as possible the benefits of similar agreements which may at any time be in force between such Contracting States and non- contracting States.

Chapter V: Administrative Measures

Article 25. -Administrative assistance

1. When the exercise of a right by a refugee would normally require the assistance of authorities of a foreign country to whom he cannot have recourse, the Contracting States in whose territory he is residing shall arrange that such assistance be afforded to him by their own authorities or by an international authority.
2. The authority or authorities mentioned in paragraph I shall deliver or cause to be delivered under their supervision to refugees such documents or certifications as would normally be delivered to aliens by or through their national authorities.
3. Documents or certifications so delivered shall stand in the stead of the official instruments delivered to aliens by or through their national authorities, and shall be given credence in the absence of proof to the contrary.

4. Subject to such exceptional treatment as may be granted to indigent persons, fees may be charged for the services mentioned herein, but such fees shall be moderate and commensurate with those charged to nationals for similar services.

5. The provisions of this article shall be without prejudice to articles 27 and 28.

*Article 26. - **Freedom of movement***

Each Contracting State shall accord to refugees lawfully in its territory the right to choose their place of residence and to move freely within its territory subject to any regulations applicable to aliens generally in the same circumstances.

*Article 27. - **Identity papers***

The Contracting States shall issue identity papers to any refugee in their territory who does not possess a valid travel document.

*Article 28. - **Travel documents***

1. The Contracting States shall issue to refugees lawfully staying in their territory travel documents for the purpose of travel outside their territory, unless compelling reasons of national security or public order otherwise require, and the provisions of the Schedule to this Convention shall apply with respect to such documents. The Contracting States may issue such a travel document to any other

refugee in their territory; they shall in particular give sympathetic consideration to the issue of such a travel document to refugees in their territory who are unable to obtain a travel document from the country of their lawful residence.

2. Travel documents issued to refugees under previous international agreements by Parties thereto shall be recognized and treated by the Contracting States in the same way as if they had been issued pursuant to this article.

Article 29. - Fiscal charges

1. The Contracting States shall not impose upon refugees duties, charges or taxes, of any description whatsoever, other or higher than those which are or may be levied on their nationals in similar situations.
2. Nothing in the above paragraph shall prevent the application to refugees of the laws and regulations concerning charges in respect of the issue to aliens of administrative documents including identity papers.

Article 30. - Transfer of assets

1. A Contracting State shall, in conformity with its laws and regulations, permit refugees to transfer assets which they have brought into its territory, to another country where they have been admitted for the purposes of resettlement.
2. A Contracting State shall give sympathetic consideration to the application of refugees for permission to transfer assets wherever they may be

and which are necessary for their resettlement in another country to which they have been admitted.

Article 31. - Refugees unlawfully in the country of refugee

1. The Contracting States shall not impose penalties, on account of their illegal entry or presence, on refugees who, coming directly from a territory where their life or freedom was threatened in the sense of article 1, enter or are present in their territory without authorization, provided they present themselves without delay to the authorities and show good cause for their illegal entry or presence.

2. The Contracting States shall not apply to the movements of such refugees restrictions other than those which are necessary and such restrictions shall only be applied until their status in the country is regularized or they obtain admission into another country. The Contracting States shall allow such refugees a reasonable period and all the necessary facilities to obtain admission into another country.

Article 32. - Expulsion

1. The Contracting States shall not expel a refugee lawfully in their territory save on grounds of national security or public order.

2. The expulsion of such a refugee shall be only in pursuance of a decision reached in accordance with due process of law. Except where compelling reasons of national security otherwise require, the refugee shall be allowed to submit evidence to clear himself, and to appeal to and be represented for the purpose

before competent authority or a person or persons specially designated by the competent authority.

3. The Contracting States shall allow such a refugee a reasonable period within which to seek legal admission into another country. The Contracting States reserve the right to apply during that period such internal measures as they may deem necessary.

Article 33. - Prohibition of expulsion or return ("refoulement")

1. No Contracting State shall expel or return ("refouler") a refugee in any manner whatsoever to the frontiers of territories where his life or freedom would be threatened on account of his race, religion, nationality, membership of a particular social group or political opinion.

2. The benefit of the present provision may not, however, be claimed by a refugee whom there are reasonable grounds for regarding as a danger to the security of the country in which he is, or who, having been convicted by a final judgement of a particularly serious crime, constitutes a danger to the community of that country.

Article 34. - Naturalization

The Contracting States shall as far as possible facilitate the assimilation and naturalization of refugees. They shall in particular make every effort to expedite naturalization proceedings and to reduce as far as possible the charges and costs of such proceedings.

Chapter VI: Executory and Transitory Provisions

Article 35. - Co-operation of the national authorities with the United Nations

1. The Contracting States undertake to co-operate with the Office of the United Nations High Commissioner for Refugees, or any other agency of the United Nations which may succeed it, in the exercise of its functions, and shall in particular facilitate its duty of supervising the application of the provisions of this Convention.

2. In order to enable the Office of the High Commissioner or any other agency of the United Nations which may succeed it, to make reports to the competent organs of the United Nations, the Contracting States undertake to provide them in the appropriate form with information and statistical data requested concerning:

   (a) The condition of refugees,

   (b) The implementation of this Convention, and

   (c) Laws, regulations and decrees which are, or may hereafter be, in force relating to refugees.

Article 36. - Information on national legislation

The Contracting States shall communicate to the Secretary-General of the United Nations the laws and regulations which they may adopt to ensure the application of this Convention.

Article 37. - Relation to previous conventions

Without prejudice to article 28, paragraph 2, of this Convention, this Convention replaces, as between Parties to it, the Arrangements of 5 July 1922, 31 May 1924, 12 May 1926, 30 June 1928 and 30 July 1935, the Conventions of 28 October 1933 and 10 February 1938, the Protocol of 14 September 1939 and the Agreement of 15 October 1946.

Chapter VII: Final Clauses

Article 38. - Settlement of disputes

Any dispute between Parties to this Convention relating to its interpretation or application, which cannot be settled by other means, shall be referred to the International Court of Justice at the request of any one of the parties to the dispute.

Article 39. - Signature, ratification and accession

1. This Convention shall be opened for signature at Geneva on 28 July 1951 and shall thereafter be deposited with the Secretary-General of the United Nations. It shall be open for signature at the European Office of the United Nations from 28 July to 31 August 1951 and shall be re-opened for signature at the Headquarters of the United Nations from 17 September 1951 to 31 December 1952.
2. This Convention shall be open for signature on behalf of all States Members of the United Nations, and also

on behalf of any other State invited to attend the Conference of Plenipotentiaries on the Status of Refugees and Stateless Persons or to which an invitation to sign will have been addressed by the General Assembly. It shall be ratified and the instruments of ratification shall be deposited with the Secretary-General of the United Nations.

3. This Convention shall be open from 28 July 1951 for accession by the States referred to in paragraph 2 of this article. Accession shall be effected by the deposit of an instrument of accession with the Secretary-General of the United Nations.

Article 40. - Territorial application clause

1. Any State may, at the time of signature, ratification or accession, declare that this Convention shall extend to all or any of the territories for the international relations of which it is responsible. Such a declaration shall take effect when the Convention enters into force for the State concerned.

2. At any time thereafter any such extension shall be made by notification addressed to the Secretary-General of the United Nations and shall take effect as from the ninetieth day after the day of receipt by the Secretary- General of the United Nations of this notification, or as from the date of entry into force of the Convention for the State concerned, whichever is the later.

3. With respect to those territories to which this Convention is not extended at the time of signature, ratification or accession, each State concerned shall consider the possibility of taking the necessary steps

in order to extend the application of this Convention to such territories, subject, where necessary for constitutional reasons, to the consent of the Governments of such territories.

Article 41. - Federal clause

In the case of a Federal or non-unitary State, the following provisions shall apply:

(a) With respect to those articles of this Convention that come within the legislative jurisdiction of the federal legislative authority, the obligations of the Federal Government shall to this extent be the same as those of parties which are not Federal States;

(b) With respect to those articles of this Convention that come within the legislative jurisdiction of constituent States, provinces or cantons which are not, under the constitutional system of the Federation, bound to take legislative action, the Federal Government shall bring such articles with a favourable recommendation to the notice of the appropriate authorities of States, provinces or cantons at the earliest possible moment;

(c) A Federal State Party to this Convention shall, at the request of any other Contracting State transmitted through the Secretary-General of the United Nations, supply a statement of the law and practice of the Federation and its constituent units in regard to any particular provision of the Convention showing the extent to which effect has been given to that provision by legislative or other action.

Article 42. - Reservations

1. At the time of signature, ratification or accession, any State may make reservations to articles of the Convention other than to articles 1, 3, 4, 16 (1), 33, 36-46 inclusive.

2. Any State making a reservation in accordance with paragraph I of this article may at any time withdraw the reservation by a communication to that effect addressed to the Secretary-General of the United Nations.

Article 43. - Entry into force

1. This Convention shall come into force on the ninetieth day following the day of deposit of the sixth instrument of ratification or accession.

2. For each State ratifying or acceding to the Convention after the deposit of the sixth instrument of ratification or accession, the Convention shall enter into force on the ninetieth day following the date of deposit by such State of its instrument of ratification or accession.

Article 44. - Denunciation

1. Any Contracting State may denounce this Convention at any time by a notification addressed to the Secretary-General of the United Nations.

2. Such denunciation shall take effect for the Contracting State concerned one year from the date upon which it is received by the Secretary-General of the United Nations.

3. Any State which has made a declaration or notification under article 40 may, at any time thereafter, by a notification to the Secretary-General of the United Nations, declare that the Convention shall cease to extend to such territory one year after the date of receipt of the notification by the Secretary-General.

Article 45. - Revision

1. Any Contracting State may request revision of this Convention at any time by a notification addressed to the Secretary-General of the United Nations.
2. The General Assembly of the United Nations shall recommend the steps, if any, to be taken in respect of such request.

Article 46. -Notifications by the Secretary-General of the United Nations

The Secretary-General of the United Nations shall inform all Members of the United Nations and non-member States referred to in article 39:

(a) Of declarations and notifications in accordance with section B of article 1;

(b) Of signatures, ratifications and accessions in accordance with article 39;

(c) Of declarations and notifications in accordance with article 40;

(d) Of reservations and withdrawals in accordance with article 42;

(e) Of the date on which this Convention will come into force in accordance with article 43;

(f) Of denunciations and notifications in accordance with article 44;

(g) Of requests for revision in accordance with article 45.

IN FAITH WHEREOF the undersigned, duly authorized, have signed this Convention on behalf of their respective Governments.

DONE at Geneva, this twenty-eighth day of July, one thousand nine hundred and fifty-one, in a single copy, of which the English and French texts are equally authentic and which shall remain deposited in the archives of the United Nations, and certified true copies of which shall be delivered to all Members of the United Nations and to the non-member States referred to in article 39.

10

Draft Declaration on the Rights of Indigenous Peoples

Draft declaration as agreed upon by the members of the working group at its eleventh session

Affirming that indigenous peoples are equal in dignity and rights to all other peoples, while recognizing the rights of all peoples to be different, to consider themselves different, and to be respected as such,

Affirming also that all peoples contribute to the diversity and richness of all civilizations and cultures, which constitute a common heritage of humankind,

Affirming further that all doctrines, polices and practices based on or advocating superiority of peoples or individuals on the basis of national origin, racial, religious, ethnic or cultural differences are racist, scientifically false, legally invalid, morally condemnable and socially unjust,

Reaffirming also that indigenous peoples, in the exercise of their rights, should be free from discrimination of any kind,

Concerned that indigenous peoples have been deprived of their human rights and fundamental freedoms, resulting, inter alia, in their colonization and the dispossession of their lands, territories and resources, thus preventing them from exercising, in particular, their right to development in accordance with their own needs and interests,

Recognizing the urgent need to respect and promote the rights and characteristics of indigenous peoples, especially their rights to their lands, territories and resources, which derive from their political, economic and social structures and from their cultures, spiritual traditions, histories and philosophies,

Welcoming the fact that indigenous peoples are organizing themselves for political, economic, and social and cultural enhancement and in order to bring an end to all forms of discrimination and oppression wherever they occur,

Convinced that control by indigenous peoples over developments affecting them and their lands, territories and resources will enable them to maintain and strengthen their institutions, cultures and traditions, and to promote their development in accordance with their aspirations and needs,

Recognizing also that respect for indigenous knowledge, cultures and traditional practices contributes to sustainable and equitable development and proper management of the environment,

Emphasizing the need for demilitarization of the lands and territories of indigenous peoples, which will contribute to peace, economic and social progress and development, understanding and friendly relations among nations and peoples of the world,

Recognizing in particular the right of indigenous families and communities to retain shared responsibility for the upbringing, training, education and well-being of their children,

Recognizing also that indigenous peoples have the right freely to determine their relationships with States in a spirit of coexistence, mutual benefit and full respect,

Considering that treaties, agreements and other arrangements between States and indigenous peoples are properly matters of international concern and responsibility,

Acknowledging that the Charter of United Nations, the International Covenant on Economic, Social and Cultural Rights and the International Covenant on Civil and political Rights affirm the fundamental importance of the right of self-determination of all peoples, by virtue of which they freely determine their political status and freely pursue their economic, social and cultural development,

Bearing in mind that nothing in this Declaration may be used to deny any peoples their right of self-determination,

Encouraging States to comply with and effectively implement all international instruments, in particular those relating to human rights, as they apply to indigenous peoples, in consultation and cooperation with the people concerned,

Emphasizing that the United Nations has an important and continuing role to play in promoting and protecting the rights of indigenous peoples,

Believing that this Declaration is a further important step forward for the recognition, promotion and protection of the rights and freedoms of indigenous peoples and in the development of relevant activities of the United Nations system in this field,

Solemnly proclaims the following United Nations Declaration on the Rights of Indigenous Peoples:

Part I

Article 1.

Indigenous peoples have the right to the full and effective enjoyment of all of the human rights and fundamental freedoms which are recognized in the Charter of the United Nations and in the human rights law;

Article 2.

Indigenous individuals and peoples are free and equal to all other individuals and peoples in dignity and rights, and have the right to be free from any kind of adverse discrimination, in particular that based on their indigenous origin or identity;

Article 3.

Indigenous people have the right of self-determination. By virtue of that right they freely determine their political status and freely pursue their economic, social and cultural development:

Article 4.

Indigenous peoples have the right to maintain and strengthen their distinct political, economic, social and cultural characteristics, as well as their legal systems, while retaining their rights to participate fully, if they so choose, in the political, economic, social and cultural life of the State;

Article 5.

Every Indigenous person has the right to belong to a nationality;

Part II

Article 6.

No Genecide Indigenous peoples have the collective right to live in freedom, peace and security as distinct peoples and to full guarantees against genocide or any other act of violence, including the removal of indigenous children from their families and communities under any pretext.

Article 7.

Indigenous peoples have the collective and individual right not to be subject to ethnocide and cultural genocide, including the prevention of and redress for:

(a) Any action which has the aim or effect of depriving them of their integrity as distinct peoples, or of their cultural values or identities;

(b) Any action which has the aim or effect of dispossessing them of their lands, territories or resources;

(c) Any form of population transfer which has the aim or effect of violating or undermining any of their rights;

(d) Any form of assimilation or integration by other cultures or ways of life imposed on them by legislative, administrative or other measures;

(e) Any form of propoganda directed against them;

Article 8.

Indigenous peoples have the collective and individual right to maintain and develop their distinct identities and characteristics, including the right to identify themselves as indigenous and to be recognized as such;

Article 9.

Indigenous peoples and individuals have the right to belong to an indigenous community or nation, in accordance with the traditions and customs of the community or nation concerned. No disadvantage of any kind may arise from the exercise of such a right;

Article 10.

Indigenous peoples shall not be forced from their lands or territories. No relocation shall take place without the free and informed consent of the indigenous peoples concerned and after agreement on just and fair compensation and, where possible, with the option of return;,

Article 11.

Indigenous peoples have the right to special protection and security in periods of armed conflict.

States shall observe international standards, in particular the Fourth Geneva Convention of 1949, for the protection of civilian populations in circumstances of emergency and armed conflict, and shall not:

(a) Recruit indigenous individuals against their will in the armed forces and, in particular, for use against other indigenous peoples;

(b) Recruit indigenous children into the armed forces under any circumstances;

(c) Force indigenous individuals to abandon their lands, territories or means of subsistence, or relocate them in special centers for military purposes;

(d) Force indigenous individuals to work for military purposes under any discriminary conditions;

Part II

Article 12.

Indigenous peoples have the right to practice and revitalize their cultural traditions and customs. This includes the right to maintain, protect and develop the past, present and future manifestations of their cultures, such as archaeological and historical sites, artifacts, designs, ceremonies, technologies and visual and performing arts and literature, as well as the right to restitution of cultural, intellectual, religious and spiritual property taken without their free and informed consent or in violation of their laws, traditions and customs;

Article 13.

Indigenous peoples have the right to manifest, practice, develop and teach their spiritual and religious traditions, customs and ceremonies; the right to maintain, protect, and have access in privacy to their religious and cultural sites; the right to use and control of ceremonial objects; and the right to repatriation of human remains.

States shall take effective measures, in conjunction with the indigenous peoples concerned, to ensure that indigenous sacred places, including burial sites, be preserved, respected and protected;

Article 14.

Indigenous peoples have the right to revitalize, use, develop and transmit to future generations their histories, languages, oral traditions, philosophies, writing systems and literatures, and to designate and retain their own names for communities, places and persons.

States shall take effective measures, especially whenever any right of indigenous peoples may be affected, to ensure this right and to ensure that they can understand and be understood in political, legal and administrative proceedings where necessary through the provision of interpretation or by other appropriate means;

Part IV

Article 15.

Indigenous children have the right to all levels and forms of education of the State. All indigenous peoples also have this right and the right to establish and control their educational systems and institutions providing education in their own languages, in a manner appropriate to their cultural methods of teaching and learning.

Indigenous children living outside their communities have the right to be provided access to education in their own culture and language.

Article 16.

Indigenous peoples have the right to have the dignity and diversity of their cultures, traditions, histories and aspirations appropriately reflected in all forms of education and public information.

States shall take effective measures, in consultation with the indigenous peoples concerned, to eliminate all prejudice and discrimination and to promote tolerance, understanding and good relations among indigenous peoples and all segments of society;

Article 17.

Indigenous people have the right to establish their own languages. They also have the right to equal access to all forms of non-indigenous media.

States shall take effective measures to ensure that State-owned media duly reflect indigenous cultural diversity;

Article 18.

Indigenous peoples have the right to enjoy fully all rights established under international labour law and national labour legislation.

Indigenous individuals have the right not to be subjected to any discriminatory conditions of labour, inter alia, employment and salary;

Part V

Article 19.

Indigenous peoples have the right to participate fully, if they so choose, at all levels of decision-making in matters which may affect their rights, lives and destinies through representatives chosen by themselves in accordance with their own procedures as well as to maintain and develop their own indigenous decision-making institutions;

Article 20.

Indigenous peoples have the right to participate fully, if they so choose, through procedures determined by them, in devising legislative or administrative measures that may affect them.

States shall obtain the free and informed consent of the peoples concerned before adopting and implementing such measures;

Article 21.

Indigenous people have the right to maintain and develop their political, economic and social systems, to be secure in the enjoyment of their own means of subsistence and development, and to engage freely in all their traditional and other economic activities. Indigenous peoples who have been deprived of their means of subsistence and development are entitled to just and fair compensation;

Article 22.

Indigenous people have the right to special measures for immediate effective and continuing improvement of their economic and social conditions, including in the areas of employment, vocational training and retraining, housing, sanitation, health and social security.

Particular attention shall be paid to the rights and special needs of indigenous elders, women, youth, children and disabled persons;

Article 23.

Indigenous people have the right to determine and develop priorities and strategies for exercising their right to development. In particular, indigenous people have the right to determine and develop all health, housing and other economic and social programmes affecting them and, as far as possible, to administer such programmes through their own institutions;

Article 24.

They also have the right to access, without any discrimination, to all medical institutions, health services and medical care;

Part VI

Article 25.

Indigenous peoples have the right to maintain and strengthen their distinctive spiritual and material relationship with the lands, territories, waters and coastal seas and other resources which they have traditionally owned or otherwise occupied or used, and to uphold their responsibilities to future generations in this regard;

Article 26.

Indigenous peoples have the right to own, develop, control and use the lands and territories, including to total environment of the lands, air, waters, coastal seas, sea-ice, flora and fauna and other resources which they have traditionally owned or otherwise occupied or used. This includes the right to the full recognition of their laws, traditions and customs, land-tenure systems and institutions for the development and management of resources, and the right to effective measures by States to prevent any interference with, alienation of or encoachment upon these rights;

Article 27.

Indigenous peoples have the right to the resititution of the lands, territories and resources which they have traditionally owned or otherwise occupied or used, and which have been confiscated, occupied, used or damaged without their free and informed consent. Where this is not possible, they have the right to just and fair compensation. Unless otherwise freely agreed upon by the peoples concerned, compensation shall take the form of lands, territories and resources equal in quality, size and legal status.

Article 28.

Indigenous peoples have the right to the conservation, restoration and protection of the total environment and production capacity of their lands, territories and resources, as well as to the assistance for this purpose from States and through international cooperation. Military activities shall not take place in the lands and territories of indigenous peoples, unless otherwise freely agreed upon by the peoples concerned.

States shall take effective measure to ensure, as needed, that programmes for monitoring, maintaining and restoring health of indigenous peoples, as developed and implemented by the peoples affected by such materials, are duly implemented;

Article 29.

Indigenous peoples are entitled to the recognition of the full ownership, control and protection of their cultural and intellectual property.

They have the right to special measures to control, develop and protect their sciences, technologies and cultural manifestations, including human and other genetic resources, seeds, medicines, knowledge of properties of fauna and flora, oral traditions, literatures, designs and visual and performing arts;

Article 30.

Indigenous peoples have the right to determine and develop priorities and strategies for the development or use of their lands, territories and other resources, including the right to require that States obtain their free and informed consent prior to the approval of any project affecting their lands, territories and other resources, particularly in connection with the development, utilization or exploitation of mineral, water or other resources. Pursuant to agreements with the indigenous peoples concerned, just and fair compensation shall be provided for any such activities and measures taken to mitigate adverse environmental, economic, social, cultural or spiritual impact;

Part VII

Article 31.

Indigenous peoples, as a specific form of exercising their right to self determination, have the right to autonomy or self-government in matters relating to their internal and local affairs, including culture, religion, education, information, media, health, housing, employment, social welfare, economic activities, land and resource management, environment and entry by non-members, as well as ways and means for financing these autonomous functions.

Article 32.

Indigenous peoples have the collective right to determine their own citizenship in accordance with their customs and traditions. Indigenous citizenship does not impair the right of indigenous individuals to obtain citizenship of the States in which they live.

Indigenous peoples have the right to determine the structures and to select the membership of their institutions in accordance with their own procedures.

Article 33.

Indigenous peoples have the right to promote, develop and maintain their institutional structures and their distinctive juridical customs, traditions, procedures and practices, in accordance with internationally recognized human right standards.

Article 34.

Indigenous peoples have the collective right to determine the responsibilities of individuals to their communities.

Article 35.

Indigenous peoples, in particular those divided by international borders, have the right to maintain and develop contacts, relations and cooperation, including activities for spiritual, cultural, political, economic and social purposes, with other peoples across the borders.

States shall take effective measures to ensure the exercise and implementation of this right.

Article 36.

Indigenous peoples have the right to the recognition, observance and enforcement of treaties, agreements and other constructive arrangements concluded with States or their successors, according to their original spirit and intent, and to have States honour and respect such treaties, agreements and other constructive arrangements. Conflicts and disputes which cannot otherwise be settled should be submitted to competent international bodies agreed to by all parties concerned;

Part VIII

Article 37.

States shall take effective and appropriate measures, in consultation with the indigenous peoples concerned, to give full effect to the provisions of this Declaration. The rights recognized herein shall be adopted and included in national legislation in such a manner that indigenous peoples can avail themselves of such rights in practice.

Article 38.

Indigenous people have the right to have access to adequate financial and technicial assistance, from States and through international cooperation, to pursue freely their political, economic, social, cultural and spiritual development and for the enjoyment of the rights and freedoms recognized in this Declaration.

Article 39.

Indigenous peoples have the right to have access to and prompt decision through mutually acceptable and fair procedures for the resolution of conflicts and disputes with the states, as well as to effective remedies for all infringements of their individual and collective rights. Such a decision shall take into consideration the customs, traditions, rules and legal systems of the indigenous peoples concerned.

Article 40.

The organs and specialized agencies of the United Nations system and other intergovernmental organizations shall contribute to the full realization of the provisions of this Declaration through the mobilization, *inter alia* , of financial cooperation and technical assistance. Ways and means of ensuring participation of indigenous peoples on issues affecting them shall be established.

Article 41.

The United Nations shall take the necessary steps to ensure the implementation of this Declaration including the creation of a body at the highest level with special competence in this field and with the direct participation of indigenous peoples. All United Nations bodies shall promote respect for and full application of the provisions of this Declaration.

Part IX

Article 42.

The rights recognized herein constitute the minimum standards for the survival, dignity and well-being of the indigenous peoples of the world.

Article 43.

All the rights and freedoms recognized herein are equally garanteed to male and female indigenous individuals.

Article 44.

Nothing in this Declaration may be construed as diminishing or extinguishing or future rights of indigenous peoples may have or acquire.

Article 45.

Nothing in this Declaration may be interpreted as implying for any State, group or person any right to engage in any activity or to perform any act contrary to the Charter of the United Nations.

Bibliography

Berman, Marshall, 'Modernism and Human Rights Near New Millennium', *Dissent*, 1995.

Cleveland, Harlan, 'The Internationalisation of Internal Affairs' in *Human Dignity* Ed. Henkin, A. H., Aspen Institute for Humanistic Studies, New York, 1979.

Cranston, *What are Human Rights?*, The Bodely Head, 1973.

Cranston, *What are Human Rights?*, The Bodely Head, 1973.

Donnelly, Jack, *Universal Human Rights in Theory and Practice*, Ithaca: Cornell University Press, 1989.

Drost, N. Pieter, *Human Rights As Legal Rights*, A.W. Sijthoft-Leyden, 1965.

Evan Luard, *International Protection of Human Rights* (1967) 14, 15 and 25.

Friedmann, W., *The Changing Structure of International Law*, Columbia University Press, New York, 1964.

Gewirth, Allan, "Why There Are Human Rights", *Social Theory and Practice*, 1985.

Harold, J. Laski, 'Towards a Universal Declaration of Human Rights', in UNESCO *Human Rights Comments and Interpretations* (London: Wingate, 1949), reproduced in *Human Rights Teaching* (UNESCO), Vol. IV, 1985.

Henkin, A. H., Ed. *Human Dignity: The Internationalisation of Human Rights*, Aspen Institute for Humanistic Studies, New York, 1979.

Human Rights Watch Global Report on Women's Human Rights, New York, 1993 and 1995.

Husak, Douglas, "The Motivation for Human Rights", *Social Theory and Practice*, 1985.

Kalaiah, A.B., *Human Rights in International Law*, 1986.

Paine, Thomas, *The Rights of Man*, New York: Penguin Books, 1985.

Peters J. and A. Wolper., *Human Rights: International Feminist Perspectives*, edited by Roudedge, New York, 1995.

Piggozzi, Mary Joy, *Implications of the Convention on the Rights of the Child for Education Activities Supported by UNICEF*, UNICEF, New York, March 1997.

Report on the Third International Human Rights Conference, Riga, Latvia, 1997.

Singh, Nagendra, *The Role and Record of the UN High Commissioner for Refugees*, Macmillan India Ltd., New Delhi, 1984, p.74.

United Nations Commission on Human Rights, *Report of the Working Group on Contemporary Forms of Slavery* (Geneva): Annual Reports, see especially 1985-87.

Index